God the Spirit

Wesleyan Doctrine Series

The Wesleyan Doctrine Series seeks to reintroduce Christians in the Wesleyan tradition to the beauty of doctrine. The volumes in the series draw on the key sources for Wesleyan teaching: Scripture, Liturgy, Hymnody, the General Rules, the Articles of Religion and various Confessions. In this sense, it seeks to be distinctively Wesleyan. But it does this with a profound interest and respect for the unity and catholicity of Christ's body, the church, which is also distinctly Wesleyan. For this reason, the series supplements the Wesleyan tradition with the gifts of the church catholic, ancient, and contemporary. The Wesleyan tradition cannot survive without a genuine "Catholic Spirit." These volumes are intended for laity who have a holy desire to understand the faith they received at their baptism.

Editors:
Randy Cooper
Andrew Kinsey
D. Brent Laytham
D. Stephen Long

God the Spirit

*Introducing Pneumatology in
Wesleyan and Ecumenical Perspective*

BETH FELKER JONES

With Questions for Consideration by Andrew Kinsey

CASCADE *Books* • Eugene, Oregon

GOD THE SPIRIT
Introducing Pneumatology in Wesleyan
and Ecumenical Perspective

Wesleyan Doctrine Series 5

Copyright © 2014 Beth Felker Jones. All rights reserved. Except for brief quotations in critical publications or reviews, no part of this book may be reproduced in any manner without prior written permission from the publisher. Write: Permissions, Wipf and Stock Publishers, 199 W. 8th Ave., Suite 3, Eugene, OR 97401.

Cascade Books
An Imprint of Wipf and Stock Publishers
199 W. 8th Ave., Suite 3
Eugene, OR 97401

www.wipfandstock.com

ISBN 13: 9781498215893

Cataloging-in-Publication data:

Jones, Beth Felker, 1976–

God the spirit : introducing pneumatology in wesleyan and ecumenical perspective / Beth Felker Jones ; with Andrew Kinsey.

x + 132 p. ; 23 cm. —Includes bibliographical references.

Wesleyan Doctrine Series 5

ISBN 13: 9781498215893

1. Holy Spirit. 2. Methodist Church—Doctrines. I. Kinsey, Andrew. II. Title. III. Series.

BX8331.3 .J66 2014

*For VTS and my Bible study group,
Spirit-filled women all.
Thanks.*

Contents

Acknowledgments ix

Introduction 1

- *one*   The Lord, the Giver of Life 7
- *two*   The Spirit in Unity with the Father and the Son 19
- *three* Being Spirit, Being Spiritual 35
- *four* Life in the Spirit 49
- *five* The Spirit and the Wesleyan *Via Salutis* 61
- *six*   The Sanctifying Spirit Will Perfect Us in Love 77
- *seven* Pentecostal Power, Global Revival, Wildness, and Order 89
- *eight* Inspiration, Illumination, and the Spirit in the Church 103
- *nine* Testing the Spirits 117

Bibliography 129

Acknowledgments

Writing about the Spirit tends, I have been delighted to find, to move one to gratitude. Here, I am grateful to those who helped make this volume possible: to the editors of the series for the invitation to write, to the team at Cascade Books, to Andy Kinsey for the discussion questions, and to friends and colleagues who have discussed aspects of this work with me and read parts or, in heroic cases, the whole: Jeff Barbeau, Tiffany Kriner, Greg Lee, Dan Treier. Especial thanks to my incomparable research assistants: Ella Myer for keeping my books and life in order and acting as a sounding board for ideas, and James Gordon for his meticulous work on citations. Thanks also to my undergraduate students, whose excellent questions about and, more importantly, relationships with the Spirit have shaped this volume. Thanks are always due to my family, for their support of my writing, for being means of grace to me.

Introduction

If we Christians measured our attention to the Holy Spirit by counting up references in sermons, prayers, and hymns, my guess is that we would find far fewer references to the Spirit than we would to Jesus, salvation, or even—most mysterious of doctrines—the Trinity. In the big picture, we seem to talk less about the Spirit than we do about other matters of faith, and so it is often claimed that the doctrine of the Holy Spirit is the most neglected of all Christian teachings.[1] Certainly, it can be an uncomfortable doctrine, one filled with mystery and burdened with anxieties. If we add to this the astonishing, even bewildering, variety of experiences Christians associate with the Holy Spirit—ranging from the cataclysmic tongue of fire to the stillest, smallest voice—perhaps it is no wonder that the doctrine has sometimes been pushed to the edges of Christian teaching.

Some of this reticence is probably warranted as appropriate awe in the face of mystery. Some of it may reflect a proper sort of silence in light of the holiness and transcendence of God, but there are also terrible reasons

1. Thus the title of Francis Chan's popular book, *Forgotten God: Reversing Our Tragic Neglect of the Holy Spirit.*

for failing to speak of the Spirit, reasons rooted in sin and in fear. In sin, we prefer the selfish life to the life of the Spirit, and, in sin, we are wont to turn our backs on the comfort offered by the Spirit of God. In fear, we shrink back from the possibility that the Spirit might do something radically new in our lives, might call us to ministry in places we do not want to go to, or bid us love people we do not want to love.

Thankfully, the Spirit works in us against this sin and this fear. The Spirit is one who casts out fear, a Spirit not "of cowardice, but rather a spirit of power and of love and of self-discipline" (2 Tim 1:7). Mercifully, the same Spirit offers us a new life, in which sin is defeated through the power of Jesus Christ, and "the law of the Spirit of life in Christ Jesus" sets us "free from the law of sin and of death" (Rom 8:2). In short, because of who the Spirit is, we may approach the study of doctrine with confidence, faith, and joyous anticipation. I pray that the Spirit of holiness and courage will use the introduction to the doctrine outlined in this book to call us, in joy, to know and love God more.

My approach to the doctrine of the Holy Spirit in this book is both broad and specific, ecumenical and Wesleyan. I speak from my location in the particular church context of the Wesleyan tradition and in the wider, ecumenical context of the whole people of God. Even this move is quite Wesleyan, for John Wesley famously advocated that Christians seek a "catholic spirit," a spirit that recognizes the work of God, not only in each particular context, but also in the church as a whole.[2]

2. J. Wesley, "Catholic Spirit," 346–55.

Introduction

Ecumenical theology draws on the wide resources of the whole church—across continents, centuries, and traditions—as it seeks unity among the people of God. The word *ecumenical* means "the whole world," and any understanding of Christian faith that ignores the ecumenical church risks, among other things, insular blindness. Where God's people have strong ecumenical agreement about doctrine, we tend to see that agreement as something brought about by the power of the Holy Spirit among us. Where the Holy Spirit, the Spirit of truth, works such consensus building, we have good reason to trust it and to hold it in high regard as a truthful expression of the faith. In Charles Wesley's Trinitarian verse:

> Shine in our hearts Father of light,
> Jesu thy beams impart,
> Spirit of truth our minds unite,
> And make us one in heart.[3]

Wesleyan theology stands in a particular historical branch of that larger church, one connected to the teachings of John Wesley as he led the Methodist movement. Christian teaching—doctrine—is, in every case, worked out both in ecumenical context and in more particular contexts, contexts that reflect the circumstances and reasoning of particular times and places and the specific needs of God's people in those places. The people of God includes a rich diversity, and different theological traditions bring their own particular beauties to the ecumenical church. Different theological traditions also respond to the needs of particular contexts, doing one of the main tasks of theology by interpreting Scripture to speak to

---

3. C. Wesley, "Universal Redemption," 315.

the circumstances of each time and place. The Wesleyan theological tradition, like all traditions, grew up in particular circumstances into which Christians tried to speak the truth of Scripture, circumstances that included a felt need for a great work of the Spirit in a church that many thought had grown complacent and cold. As a Wesleyan theologian, I continue to believe that this tradition has important gifts to offer to new times and places as well as to the ecumenical church, and I think that this is particularly true about the doctrine of the Holy Spirit.

One of the special gifts of the Wesleyan theological tradition is that it leans against any tendency to neglect the Spirit. Historically, Wesleyan Christianity has made it a practice to attend to the Spirit in ways that have not always happened in the wider church. At the same time, Wesleyan Christian teaching about the Holy Spirit stands in firm continuity with the larger, ecumenical teaching of the church. In this book, we will explore that teaching about the doctrine of pneumatology (the Greek *pneuma* means "breath" or "spirit" and so gives us the basis for this term for the doctrine of the Holy Spirit).

In the chapters that follow, I have tried to attend to pneumatology in ways that show the importance of the doctrine to our understanding of Christian faith and life. Chapter 1 begins with the teaching of the early church that the Spirit is the "Lord" and the "giver of life." This teaching recognizes that the Spirit is truly God and, as the third person of the Trinity, is always related to the Father and the Son even as he (more about this personal pronoun in chapter 2) relates to us as God's children. The second chapter draws attention to the relationships between the Father, the Son, and the Spirit. In this chapter,

Introduction

I pay close attention to clues we get about those relationships in Scripture. Chapter 3 is about what it means to be spiritual in relationship to a God who is spirit, and I raise questions about the relationship between human beings, who are embodied creatures, and the Spirit, who is ineffable God. Our life in the Spirit—full of the fruit of the Spirit—is the topic of chapter 4. The fifth chapter explores the work of the Spirit in salvation, addressing Wesleyan theological emphases, and chapter 6 continues the story of salvation as we look at the Spirit's work in perfecting us in love. In chapter 7, I address questions about what we as Christians are to make of the sometime unruliness that goes along with the Spirit's work, questions about the gifts of the Spirit, both wild and ordinary, poured out on all God's people. Chapter 8 considers the Spirit's work in the church and in the Scriptures, and the final chapter turns to questions about discernment. My prayer is that this introduction to pneumatology will encourage us to see the Holy Spirit at work in our work, both in our individual callings as children of God and in our corporate work as the body of Christ. Taken as a whole, these nine chapters introduce key subjects in the doctrine. I hope it will draw the reader's attention to what is beautiful and life-giving therein and that it might spur us to deeper love for and openness to God the Spirit.

God the Spirit

Comments

Beth Felker Jones' commentary on the Holy Spirit provides a wonderful opportunity for persons and groups to explore a sometimes "neglected" teaching in the life of the church. Jones's summary of the Spirit builds upon a solid ecumenical foundation while also drawing out the distinctive features of a Wesleyan understanding.

The following Questions for Consideration are meant to assist readers in Jones's exploration of the Holy Spirit. They have been created to help persons and churches with the conversation the church has been having over the centuries about what the Spirit is "up to" or doing. And while the current set of questions may not exhaust all the angles of the person and work of the Spirit, they will hopefully instigate further discussion, if not action. This present commentary is one of several commentaries designed to engage the church in ongoing formation and instruction.

Andrew Kinsey

Questions for Consideration

1. "The doctrine of the Holy Spirit is the most neglected of all Christian teachings." Do you agree with this statement? Why or why not?
2. What experiences might we associate with the Holy Spirit? Do these experiences speak about why we may have a difficult time talking about the Spirit? Explain.

one

The Lord, the Giver of Life

> What then is the charge they bring against us? They accuse us of profanity for entertaining lofty conceptions about the Holy Spirit.... We, for instance, confess that the Holy Spirit is of the same rank as the Father and the Son, so that there is no difference between them in anything, to be thought or named, that devotion can ascribe to a Divine nature.... But our opponents aver that He is a stranger to any vital communion with the Father and the Son; that by reason of an essential variation He is inferior to, and less than they in every point.... He is Divine, and absolutely good, and omnipotent, and wise, and glorious, and eternal; He is everything of this kind that can be named to raise our thoughts to the grandeur of His being.... He is Himself Goodness, and Wisdom, and Power, and Sanctification, and Righteousness, and Everlastingness, and Imperishability, and every name that is lofty, and elevating above other names.[1]

---

1. Gregory of Nyssa, "On the Holy Spirit," 315.

God the Spirit

Gregory of Nyssa wrote these words against the Pneumatomachi—fighters against the Holy Spirit—a group who denied that the Spirit is truly God. Gregory insisted, to the contrary, that the Spirit is equal to, "of the same rank as," the Father and the Son and that this is the clear testimony of Scripture. Gregory is likely thinking of many aspects of Scripture, among them the remarkable testimony that "the Spirit searches everything, even the depths of God" (1 Cor 2:10). We see Gregory offering a litany of praise to the Spirit, identifying the attributes of the Spirit with the Spirit's very nature in a way that can only belong to God.

Late in the fourth century, leaders from across the church came to renewed affirmation of belief in the triune God: Father, Son, and Holy Spirit. These ecumenical leaders shared Gregory's teaching above and explicitly recognized the Spirit's divinity. The church reaffirmed the teachings of the Nicene Creed, a confession of faith that is still used across the church—in Eastern Orthodox practice, among Roman Catholics, and in many Protestant traditions. I begin with the Nicene Creed, then, as an ecumenical starting point representing the most widely shared pneumatology of the universal church. The ending of that creed treats the doctrine of the Spirit:

> We believe in the Holy Spirit, the Lord, the giver of life,
> who proceeds from the Father and the Son,
> who with the Father and the Son is worshiped
>   and glorified,
> who has spoken through the prophets.

The creed affirms that the Holy Spirit is both "Lord" and "giver of life." It recognizes the eternal relationships between Father, Son, and Spirit as we see those relationships testified to in Scripture, and it proclaims that the Spirit "with the Father and the Son is worshiped and glorified." These creedal statements form the great affirmations of ecumenical pneumatology. The rest of this chapter will begin to explore those affirmations in two movements. First, the Spirit as "Lord" and "giver of life" is none other than the true God, fully divine. Second, the Spirit is personal both in relationship to the Father and the Son and in relationship to human beings.

The Spirit Is Truly God

The truth that the Spirit is God is the most important claim about the Spirit in the early ecumenical creeds. Against detractors who would have demoted the Spirit to some quasi-divine status, the church recognized that the scriptural story of God's work in the world entails the Spirit's full divinity. Put differently, the story of Scripture makes no sense if the Spirit is not truly and really God. The creed affirms the Spirit's divine nature by granting the titles "Lord" and "life-giver," titles that Scripture demands we give to the Spirit, titles that can only properly belong to God.

At this stage of the book, I wonder: Ought I to try to sketch out the doctrine of the Trinity, the doctrine that houses the claim that the Spirit is God? For the sake of attending to pneumatology as fully as possible in a short volume, I have decided not to attempt such a sketch here, trusting my reader to other volumes in this series, but I do want to give some context for the creedal claim about the Spirit's divine nature. We need that context in order to get a sense of the astounding beauty reflected there. I will proceed, then, by laying out some reasons that it seemed, in the time leading up to these ecumenical councils, impossible that the Spirit might truly be God. Then, I will describe some of the logic that the councils accepted as refutation of those arguments.

Before the third and fourth ecumenical councils, the problem that Christians saw with the divinity of the Spirit was that of the oneness of God. It seemed impossible to affirm, at the same time, that (*a*) there is only one God and (*b*) that the Father, Son, and Spirit are all truly God. The same strange Trinitarian math puzzles Christians today. The simplest solutions involved denying the divinity—the god-ness—of the Son and the Spirit. This seemingly obvious answer, though, caused more problems than it solved. In denying the divinity of the Son or the Spirit, Christians came to see that they were violating the logic of the scriptural story of salvation. Only God is to be worshipped. Only God can save. Since Father, Son, and Spirit are all to be worshipped, since Christians are baptized in the name of all three, since all three are integral to salvation, all three must truly be God. Through painstaking work, the Christians who shaped the creed saw this clearly. Because the Spirit is "worshiped and glorified," because the Spirit gives life and salvation,[2] the Spirit is God. No watered-down version of divinity will do.

The title "Lord" respects the Spirit's divinity by placing human beings under the direction and power of the Spirit and by identifying the Spirit with the Father and

---

2. Titus 3:4; 1 Pet 1:2

The Lord, the Giver of Life

the Son. The recognition that this Lord is the "giver of life" also respects the Spirit's divinity by acknowledging that the Spirit, together with the Father and the Son, does what God does. The Spirit, in giving life, works what only God can do. There are many biblical bases for these two affirmations. Both are found together when Paul tells believers that they are living letters of recommendation, letters written by the Spirit on human hearts, and he reminds us that we find our competence and confidence, not in ourselves, but in God, clearly identified as the Spirit who "gives life" (2 Cor 3:6). Later in the same chapter, Paul presses believers to act "with great boldness" as we witness to God's glory, a boldness that is legitimated by the Lord, again clearly identified with the Spirit. "The Lord is the Spirit," Paul preaches, "and where the Spirit of the Lord is, there is freedom" (3:17). In the freedom of the Spirit of God, we are transformed and thus able to truly reflect God's image and glory. Again, "this comes from the Lord, the Spirit" (3:18). Here, Paul rejoices in the lifegiving power of God the Spirit, power that no mere creature can claim. In recognizing the full divinity of the Holy Spirit, the Wesleyan tradition stands in continuity with the ancient creed and with Scripture. This continuity is clearly displayed in the fourth of the Articles of Religion, which Wesley adopted verbatim from the Anglican articles: "The Holy Ghost, proceeding from the Father and the Son, is of one substance, majesty and glory with the Father and the Son, very and eternal God."

When we confess that the Spirit is Lord, we are also recognizing the unity of the three persons of the godhead, the intimate connection between the Father, the Son, and the Spirit. In the Old Testament, the title LORD, written just so, in all capital letters, serves as a stand-in for the holy name of God that was revealed to Moses at the burning bush:

> But Moses said to God, "If I come to the Israelites and say to them, 'The God of your ancestors has sent me to you,' and they ask me, 'What is his name?' what shall I say to them?" God said to Moses, "I AM WHO I AM." He said further, "Thus you shall say to the Israelites, 'I AM has sent me to you.'" God also said to Moses, "Thus you shall say to the Israelites, 'The LORD, the God of your ancestors, the God of Abraham, the God of Isaac, and the God of Jacob, has sent me to you': This is my name forever, and this my title for all generations." (Exod 3:13–15)

That name was held in such reverence, recognized as so holy, that it was not to be spoken, and so the title LORD stands in, in the text, for God's holy, transcendent, divine being. The church father Gregory of Nazianzus wrote that the names revealed in the third chapter of Exodus "are the special names" for God's essence, names appropriate for "a nature whose being is absolute . . . being is in its proper sense peculiar to God and belongs to him entirely."[3] In other words, this holy name indicates that God is God. When the creed makers recognized that the title "Lord" belongs not to the Father alone but to Father, Son, and Spirit, they were recognizing that all these three are the one God. All these three are of the divine essence. When the creed asserts its continuity with the prophets, it is asserting that the one God known to Israel and revealed in the Old Testament is the same one God further revealed

---

3. Gregory of Nazianzus, "Fourth Theological Oration," 316.

The Lord, the Giver of Life

in the New Testament as triune. The Spirit who came upon the prophets of old is the same Spirit who came to the early church at Pentecost and the same Spirit who works in the church today. The one God, who we know in both the Old and New Testaments, is Father, Son, and Holy Spirit. This recognition does not solve the problem of triune math. Instead, it lives with the problem and rejoices in the holy mystery it contains.

The life-giving work of the Spirit is seen throughout Scripture. It begins with the first chapter of Genesis, where Christians have traditionally seen the Spirit at work as God hovers over the waters. That life-giving work continues throughout the story of salvation, and this is affirmed in the creedal language that identifies the Holy Spirit as the same Spirit who spoke through the prophets. In the New Testament witness, the life-giving work of the Spirit is seen in special ways in connection to Jesus; it is the Spirit who is at work in the life-giving conception of Jesus in Mary's womb, who descends on Jesus at his baptism, and who, at the end of Jesus' life, works in raising him from the dead. The Spirit's life-giving work extends to us as well, both in the present, as we receive new life, and in the future, with the promise of everlasting, resurrected life. To "set the mind on the Spirit is life and peace" (Rom 8:6). The birth that Jesus told Nicodemus about is a birth "of water and the Spirit" (John 3:5), and "what is born of the Spirit is spirit" (John 3:6). Here, the beautiful imagery of life-giving birth is connected to the new life the believer receives in the Spirit.

God the Spirit

The Spirit's Personal Status

In thinking about the three persons of the Trinity, it seems obvious that the Father and the Son are personal. Father and Son are clearly relational terms. In fact, when we are talking about the Trinity, these terms make sense only in relationship to each other. The Father is the father of someone: the Son, Jesus Christ. The Son is the son of someone: his eternal father. This personal, relational language communicates quite a bit about who God is and what kind of relationships human beings can have with God. When we consider the doctrine of the Holy Spirit, though, there is a tendency to be less certain about personal language and personal relationship. The term *spirit* is not inherently relational like the terms *father* and *son*, and so we may depersonalize the Spirit. The creed testifies to the personal status of the Spirit—and to the blessed truth that we humans can relate personally to the same Spirit—when it describes the Spirit in terms of eternal relationships with the Father and the Son. The Spirit, in the Nicene Creed, "proceeds" from the Father and the Son and is worshipped and glorified together with them, indicating personal relationships of the most mutual kind.

What can it mean for the Spirit to "proceed" from the Father and the Son? This is a contested question, and it has threatened the ecumenical status of the creed. The original creedal language stated only that the Spirit "proceeds from the Father," and it indicated the eternal relationship between Father and Spirit. The phrase "and from the Son"—in Latin, *filioque*—was added to the creed in the Latin-speaking Western church over a number of years. While the Nicene Creed is still an incalculably important piece of ecumenical teaching, there is also disagreement here. The Greek-speaking East objected to—and continues to object to—the West's unilateral addition to an ecumenical creed, made without acknowledgment of or conversation with the East.

The Latin addition seems to have grown up as a way of reaffirming the full divinity of the Spirit and the Son in their eternal relationships to one another, and it stands within a tendency, in the West, to see the three persons of the Trinity in mutuality and coequality, whereas the tendency in Eastern Trinitarian theology has been to emphasize the Father as the source of the Trinity. The Wesleyan theological tradition is a tributary of the Western branch of the Christian stream, and so Wesleyan theology tends to affirm that the phrase "proceeds from the Father and the Son" is a good way to talk about the Spirit's relationships within the Trinity. This can be seen in the fourth of the Articles of Religion, on the Holy Ghost, quoted above. It might be interesting here to note that some scholars have also diagnosed deeply seated sympathies with the Eastern Orthodox theological tradition in the theology of John Wesley. While this does not put Wesleyans outside of the ecumenical controversy over the *filioque* clause, it might indicate something of the ecumenical and catholic tendencies of the Wesleyan tradition as well as something of the Wesleyan tradition's great emphasis on the Spirit, given that Western Christianity is often critiqued for failing in just that emphasis.

Certainly, the unilateral action of the Western church is no model for doing ecumenical theology, and there is a lesson here about the need for Christians to listen to one another in making doctrinal proclamation.

God the Spirit

While the East objects to the Western *filioque*, East and West still agree that the Spirit is truly God, that the Spirit exists in eternal relationship with the Father and the Son, and that the Spirit proceeds from the Father.

The term *proceeds* indicates the eternal relatedness of Father and Spirit. This relationship is one that has no creaturely parallels. The eternal relatedness of the Father, the Son, and the Spirit is a distinctive aspect of the Christian doctrine of the Trinity. Christians believe not just that God *has* relationships, but that God *is* relationship. The new birth we receive in the Spirit brings us into the relational life of God in a special way. God—Father, Son, and Holy Spirit—relates to us as beloved children. The creed also affirms that the Spirit, together with the Father and the Son, is "worshiped and glorified." This language reaffirms the full divinity of the Spirit. After all, only God is to be worshiped and glorified, and if the one we are worshipping is less than God, we have fallen into idolatry. This language also points to something about the relationship between human beings and the triune God. In this relationship, we are able to recognize and honor God because of who God is, to be included in the beauty of giving praise to the Trinity, and to be transformed into people who glorify the Lord.

The Lord, the Giver of Life

Questions for Consideration

1. Why is the claim that the "Spirit is God" considered one of the most important claims, if not the most important claim, in the early creeds of the church? What are the consequences of saying that the Spirit is not truly God?

2. Why is it important to see the person and work of the Holy Spirit in continuity with the ancient creeds and with Scripture, in both Old and New Testaments?

3. How is the life-giving power of the Spirit revealed throughout the history of salvation? What events in this history speak to God's life-giving power?

4. What does the personal status of the Spirit entail in terms of the eternal relationship of the Spirit to the Father and the Son and to us? Does the *filioque* clause matter with respect to the ways we may understand the person and work of the Spirit? Explain.

5. In this chapter we read that God does not just *have* relationships but that God *is* relationship. How is God's eternal relatedness as Father, Son, and Holy Spirit distinctively Christian, and how does such relatedness assist us in relating to God and others in both the church and the world?

two

The Spirit in Unity with the Father and the Son

In our hope to come to know the Spirit better, we turn to consider the Spirit's unity with the Father and the Son. We are at the heart of the transcendence and holiness of God here, and, as always when we seek the things of God, we do so within our human limits. No theological proposal is going to explain the mystery of the Trinity or lay bare the mysteries of the unified relationships between the Father, the Son, and the Holy Spirit. God is always more than we can imagine, beyond what we can conceive.

Blessedly, though, the holy and transcendent God has not left us in ignorance. We can, by grace and miracle, get to know this God. I will begin this chapter with several key passages in Scripture that reveal something about the mysterious relational life of a God who is three-in-one. Having explored something of what Scripture reveals about the relational unity of Spirit, Son, and Father, we will be in a place to consider two contested pneumatological questions—the question of using gendered language for the Spirit and the question of how to understand enigmatic biblical references to a sin against the Spirit. We are helped in our consideration of these questions if we attend to the unity of the Spirit with the Father and the Son.

The Spirit's Unity with the Father and the Son

The Christian doctrine of the Trinity recognizes that the one true God is, without any loss of that oneness, eternally three persons: Father, Son, and Holy Spirit. God's oneness and threeness are both revealed through the scope of the biblical narrative. One major strand of the Old Testament involves God's people learning to recognize God's oneness, the truth that there is no other God but God. While the nations around Israel assume that their gods exist alongside the gods of the other nations, Israel learns that the God who led them out of Egypt is the only God who *is*. The gods of the nations are not just inferior to the God of Israel. They are false. They do not, in reality, exist at all.

The New Testament bears witness to the one God of Israel working in hitherto unexpected ways. That one true God came to dwell among us. Jesus Christ entered into flesh, space, and time. He was born, he died, and he was raised from the dead, and all along the way, we see the incarnate God in relationship with God his Father and with God the Holy Spirit. After Jesus' resurrection, he returned to the Father, and he promised to send his Spirit to live among us. This is too simple a sketch of the story, but it was through reading and trusting in this story that God's people came to understand God as Trinity. The

The Spirit in Unity with the Father and the Son

people who had already learned, as God worked among them, that God alone is God now learned that God's oneness does not exclude threeness. The one, holy God of Israel is none other than the one triune God: Father, Son, and Holy Spirit.

We often trip over this seeming oddity in Christian doctrine. How can oneness and threeness both be the truth about God? Again, no work of theology is going to clear up the mystery here, but in the unity of the Spirit with the Father and the Son, we can learn more about the mystery of threeness and oneness together. The unity of the three persons of the Trinity is not *all* there is to say about the oneness of the three-person God, but it is certainly one of the things that we, as children of that God, will want to learn about as we seek to know him more. The Spirit's unity with the Father and the Son is clearly affirmed in the fourth of the Methodist Articles of Religion; "The Holy Ghost," for Anglican and Wesleyan theology, "proceeding from the Father and the Son is of one substance, majesty, and glory with the Father and the Son, very and eternal God."

One Pauline text, pointing to the triune unity, particularly stands out for its pneumatological underpinnings:

> These things God has revealed to us through the Spirit; for the Spirit searches everything, even the depths of God. For what human being knows what is truly human except the human spirit that is within? So also no one comprehends what is truly God's except the Spirit of God. Now we have received not the spirit of the world, but the Spirit that is from God, so that we may understand the gifts bestowed on us by God. And we speak of these things in words not taught by hu-

> man wisdom but taught by the Spirit, interpreting spiritual things to those who are spiritual. Those who are unspiritual do not receive the gifts of God's Spirit, for they are foolishness to them, and they are unable to understand them because they are spiritually discerned. Those who are spiritual discern all things, and they are themselves subject to no one else's scrutiny. "For who has known the mind of the Lord so as to instruct him?" But we have the mind of Christ. (1 Cor 2:10–16)

The claim that the Spirit searches the "depths of God" is nothing less than astonishing. None but God could do so. Even more extraordinary, more gracious, is the application of the claim to us—to human beings—as knowers of God. The Spirit of God helps us understand the gifts of God. Those who are in Christ receive, by the Spirit, the wisdom of God. So, Paul weds claims about God to claims about us. He acknowledges, at a bone-deep level, the distinction between Creator and creation. God is God, and we are not, but this difference between God and us is not the end of the story.

The holy, mysterious, majestic God, who is *not* one of us, is willing to come to us, to fill us with the Spirit, and this makes it possible for human beings, who are not God, to know the things of God, to "discern all things," to "have the mind of Christ." God the Spirit, who is *not* one of us, *is* truly—in holiness, majesty, and mystery—God, and so, only so, the communication of wisdom that we receive in the Spirit is real and true and divine. New Testament scholar Gordon Fee explains that the root of Paul's argument is "the Greek philosophic principle of 'like is known only by like,' that is, humans do not on their own pos-

The Spirit in Unity with the Father and the Son

sess the quality that would make it possible to know God or God's wisdom. Only 'like is known by like'; only God can know God. Therefore the Spirit of God becomes the link between God and humanity."[1] The Spirit is seen in unity with the Father and the Son. The gift of the "mind of Christ" is a pneumatological gift, and that same mind of Christ is one of obedience to and harmony with the will of the Father. Fee goes on to further explore the mystery of the Trinity as we glimpse it in this passage: "the closest kind of intimate, interior relationship exists between the Father and the Spirit. . . . [I]n our reception of the Spirit, we are on intimate terms with none other than God himself, personally and powerfully present, as the one who in this case reveals God's ways to us."[2]

The triune God, the living God, is three and one. This same God reveals to us that oneness and difference can truly exist together. God—Father, Son, and Holy Spirit—comprehends real difference and true oneness within the eternal, divine life. The three persons of the Trinity are truly one, united in work and in will. That oneness is so deep and true that the Spirit can search the depths of God. Just as true, the three persons of the Trinity are three. The Father is not the Son, who is not the Holy Spirit. Their difference is so real that it is not nonsense to speak of the Spirit, who is God, doing that searching—or, again in Fee's explanation of the text, the Spirit who is "not identical to the Father" knowing and revealing to us "God's thoughts, God's ways."[3] The threeness of the Father, Son, and Spirit involves the kind of

1. Fee, *God's Empowering Presence*, 99.
2. Ibid., 101.
3. Ibid.

difference that indicates true relationship in the life of the Trinity.

Theologian Kathryn Tanner plays on the same theme. "God is different from this world in virtue of the fullness of God's Trinitarian life," Tanner says. But the difference between God and the world is, in the loving will of God, filled up with the goodness of the Spirit, or, again in Tanner's words, "it is this very fullness that enables God to overflow in goodness to us. The Father already brings about what is different—the Son and the Spirit—in complete unity with the Father."[4] I hope my reader will see the beauty of Tanner's Trinitarian logic here, a logic that has implications for all the other ways we think about unity and difference. Tanner reflects on the Spirit in relationship with the Father and the Son, a relationship of true unity:

> Reinforcing the unity of being between Father and Son by a unity of love and joyful affirmation, the Holy Spirit is the exuberant, ecstatic carrier of the love of Father and Son to us. Borne by the Holy Spirit, the love of the Father for the Son is returned to the Father by the Son within the Trinity; so the triune God's manifestation in the world is completed in Christ through the work of the Spirit who enables us to return the love of God shown in Christ through a life lived in gratitude and service to God's cause.[5]

This is mind-blowing stuff, but I encourage you to read it again. Take each clause in turn, savor it, and consider it in light of the text from 1 Corinthians quoted above. God's

4. Tanner, *Jesus, Humanity, and the Trinity*, 13.
5. Ibid., 14.

The Spirit in Unity with the Father and the Son

own life is a life of oneness together with difference, of truest unity together with diversity. What is more, these features of God's life mark God's loving, personal relationship with us, a relationship in which the Spirit, who is not the Father or the Son, indwells and empowers us, helping us embody God's love for us. Unity together with diversity are features of the Christian life. In the Spirit's power, we are truly united with Christ our Lord. Because Jesus has won victory over sin, we are enabled to relate to the Spirit and the Father in ways that parallel Jesus' relationships to them during his life on earth. In the Spirit's power, the people of God are also united as one, "even as," Tanner writes, "the Holy Spirit encourages the uniqueness of our persons by a diversity of gifts of the Spirit."[6]

When thinking about the Trinity, I often encourage students to spend time studying the Gospel of John and attending to the clues we find there about the relationships between Father, Son, and Spirit. Here, I want to offer several of those suggestive texts and invite you, as you read through them, to continue to contemplate the following:

1. the Spirit's unity with the Father and the Son;
2. the Spirit's difference from the Father and the Son;
3. the ways that God's unity-together-with-difference affects our life with God.

There is endless food for thought and faith here. What do Jesus' words below suggest about the unity of the Spirit with both Jesus and the Father? What do they suggest about the Spirit's divine personhood?

6. Ibid., 83.

God the Spirit

> If you love me, you will keep my commandments. And I will ask the Father, and he will give you another Advocate, to be with you forever. This is the Spirit of truth, whom the world cannot receive, because it neither sees him nor knows him. You know him, because he abides with you, and he will be in you. I will not leave you orphaned; I am coming to you. In a little while the world will no longer see me, but you will see me; because I live, you also will live. On that day you will know that I am in my Father, and you in me, and I in you. They who have my commandments and keep them are those who love me; and those who love me will be loved by my Father, and I will love them and reveal myself to them. (John 14:15–21)

Notice the mutual relationships between the three divine persons of the Trinity, and notice how Jesus expects the love between the Father, Son, and Spirit to be manifest among us. When Jesus ascends to the Father, when we can no longer see Jesus face to face, the Father sends the Holy Spirit to us as an Advocate. In Jesus we are made children of the Father, and neither Father nor Son leaves us "orphaned." God the Holy Spirit abides with us and in us, empowering us to love. The Spirit, as the Advocate among us, will point us straight back to the Son. Jesus describes the Spirit's work in the next chapter of John's Gospel: "When the Advocate comes, whom I will send to you from the Father, the Spirit of truth who comes from the Father, he will testify on my behalf" (John 15:26). Notice how the Spirit, sent from the Father, sent by the Son, shows and testifies, not on his own behalf, but for the Son with whom he is one.

The Spirit's Work with the Father and the Son

One of the clearest Trinitarian references in the gospels is in Matthew 28, often called the "Great Commission" because, here, Jesus charges the disciples to take up his work, to go "and make disciples of all nations, baptizing them in the name of the Father and of the Son and of the Holy Spirit and teaching them to obey everything that I have commanded you" (Matt 28:19–20). In the invocation of the triune name—Father, Son, and Holy Spirit—we received the baptismal promise and calling. We are brought into the life of God, into the love shared between Father, Son, and Spirit, even as we are commissioned for obedience to Jesus and the work of disciple-making in the world.

We live in a time in which we sometimes have to look hard for Christian unity, a time in which the church has been divided and subdivided into a bewildering mass of groups and disagreements. Even in such a time, though, Christians share the one baptism referenced in Mathew 28. Across those many differences, Christians are united in the one God who is named and who acts when we receive water baptism, and that one God *is* unity, the unity of the eternal Father, the eternal Son, and the eternal Holy Spirit. Because our unity, even though we have broken it in so many ways, rests in God's unity, we have good reason to claim the words of Ephesians with confidence: "There is one body and one Spirit, just as you were called to the one hope of your calling, one Lord, one faith, one baptism, one God and Father of all, who is above all and through all and in all" (Eph 4:4–6). Bearing in mind the Spirit's unity with the Father and the Son, we are now in a place to better understand, first, the use of gendered language for the Spirit and, second, the sin against the Spirit.

Gendered Language

You may have noticed that, as I write about God, I tend to avoid using personal pronouns. When I need a personal pronoun for God, though, I have used the masculine, and this is the same rule I have followed for reference to the Holy Spirit. Because trends in contemporary theology complicate this matter, I thought about putting this note right at the beginning of this book, but I decided that it could not make sense without first considering the Spirit as the third person of the Trinity, in unity with the Father and the Son. Theologians have always reminded the church that God is more than we could ever imagine, and part of what this means is that God is beyond gender. God is neither male nor female.

In recent decades, some theologians have argued that the use of masculine pronouns for God may confuse this fact, may tempt us to anthropomorphize God—form God in our own image instead of remembering that things are the other way around, that we are made in the image of an unimaginable God. Feminist critique raises the concern that masculine language for God may contribute to the human tendency to fashion false idols, to think of God as a man. This point is absolutely right; God is not a male being in the sky. God is not pretty much like our fathers and brothers and the guys whom we know. What can the church do to work against any idolatry that would suggest otherwise?

The Spirit in Unity with the Father and the Son

Theologian Janet Soskice explains that "one strategy has been to feminize the Spirit. We can readily uncover a tradition of regarding the Spirit as the maternal aspect of God—brooding, nurturing, bringing new members of the Church to life in baptism."[7] Soskice believes that this strategy tends to fail. Feminizing the Spirit, by implication, further masculinizes the Father and the Son, and so calling the Spirit "she" inadvertently strengthens the idolatrous idea that God is a gendered being. The feminized Spirit may also strengthen cultural stereotypes about what it means to be masculine or feminine in the first place. Most importantly, in light of the triune unity outlined in this chapter, such a strategy introduces division into the Trinity; and, assuming it trades on cultural expectations that feminine means subservience, it turns the Spirit into a "helpmate to the other two Persons, who are really there to be known and loved."[8] But the Spirit is God. The Spirit, with the Father and the Son, is to be known and loved. Soskice rejects any attempt to model human gender roles on God's triune life:

> The doctrine of the Trinity tells us nothing about how men and women should relate to one another as males and females. It does not show that all men should be like the "father" and all women model themselves on a feminized Spirit. In this sense the doctrine tells us nothing about sexual difference. But it does let us glimpse what it is, most truly, to be: "to be" most fully is "to-be-related" in difference.[9]

7. Soskice, *Kindness of God*, 112.

8. Ibid., 113.

9. Ibid., 124.

God the Spirit

Masculine personal pronouns used for God are not unproblematic. This is the reason behind my practice of avoiding them where possible. At the same time, when a pronoun is called for, I think that masculine personal pronouns are the *least* problematic route. One explanation for the Old Testament use of masculine language for God is to read it as a move against idolatry. In the Canaanite context, Israel was surrounded by polytheism, by gods and goddesses. Masculine language for God rejects that context, reiterating the unity of God and the difference between God and idols.[10] In the New Testament context, masculine pronouns for God acknowledge the reality of the incarnation and the personal relationship between the Father and his Son. The God of Scripture cannot be depersonalized. We see this in the love shared between the Father, the Son, and the Spirit. To extend the natural masculine pronoun for Father and Son—he—to the Spirit as the third person of the Trinity is further acknowledgment of the triune unity and of the Spirit's personal nature. We see this implicit in the Gospel of John, where the word *Spirit*, a neuter noun in Greek, is personalized through a shift to the masculine personal pronoun. Jesus says, "When the Spirit of truth comes, he will guide you into all the truth; for he will not speak on his own, but will speak whatever he hears, and he will declare to you the things that are to come. He will glorify me, because he will take what is mine and declare it to you" (John 16:13–14). The Spirit is personal, both in his relationship to other divine persons and to us, and it will not do to call the Spirit "it." Our language for God should reflect both

---

10. See Jenson, "The Father, He . . . ," 95–109.

the unity of the Trinity and the personability of the divine persons.

To Sin against the Spirit

The unity of the Father, Son, and Holy Spirit is also the key to understanding gospel references to a great sin against the Spirit, an unforgivable sin. One account is found in the Gospel of Matthew. Jesus has just had a confrontation with the Pharisees over picking grain and healing on the Sabbath, and he has claimed his mastery over the law, saying, "the Son of Man is lord of the Sabbath" (Matt 12:8). The Pharisees attribute Jesus' healing power to Satan, charging that "it is only by Beelzebul, the ruler of the demons, that this fellow casts out demons" (12:24). It is this false charge that prompts Jesus' claims about a sin against the Spirit:

> Every kingdom divided against itself is laid waste, and no city or house divided against itself will stand. If Satan casts out Satan, he is divided against himself; how then will his kingdom stand? If I cast out demons by Beelzebul, by whom do your own exorcists cast them out? Therefore they will be your judges. But if it is by the Spirit of God that I cast out demons, then the kingdom of God has come to you. . . . Therefore I tell you, people will be forgiven for every sin and blasphemy, but blasphemy against the Spirit will not be forgiven. Whoever speaks a word against the Son of Man will be forgiven, but whoever speaks against the Holy Spirit will not be forgiven, either in this age or in the age to come. (Matt 12:25–28, 31–32)

God the Spirit

Jesus' reference to a sin that will not be forgiven does not come out of nowhere; the reference comes in the very clear context of the Pharisees' accusation. To blaspheme against the Spirit is to say that Jesus' power is not from God. It is, finally, to refuse to acknowledge Jesus as "the way, the truth, and the life" (John 14:6), the one who is "Lord of the Sabbath" and full of the Spirit's power. It makes no sense outside of the unity of the Father, Son, and Spirit. Christians sometimes worry that they might accidentally commit the "unforgivable sin," but what we learn, here and elsewhere in the New Testament, is that we need not fear. To be in Christ and to acknowledge his Lordship is already to be united with the Spirit. To be in Christ is, by grace, to be forgiven of all sin. To sin against the Spirit is to refuse God's own self—not some lesser part of God, but the one true God who has opened forgiveness to us through the work of Jesus Christ.

Questions for Consideration

1. In sharing about the "seeming oddity" of the Christian doctrine of the Trinity, Beth Felker Jones writes about the ways in which "oneness" and "threeness" are the truth about God. Is the Christian doctrine of God as Trinity an oddity? Explain.
2. How does the Spirit help us know the gifts of God?
3. How is the principle "like is known only by like" helpful when discussing our knowledge of God? How is the Holy Spirit the "link" in this knowledge?

The Spirit in Unity with the Father and the Son

4. How can the church's doctrine of the Trinity assist us in thinking about issues relating to unity and difference? What is the "food for thought" here with respect to the ways in which we as Christians are to relate to God and others?

5. What are some of the dangers of using masculine pronouns for God? What are some of the concerns with viewing the Holy Spirit solely in feminine terms? In what ways might we use language to speak appropriately of God?

6. Our language for God should reflect both the unity of the Trinity and the personality of the divine persons. Why is this important?

7. What is the unforgivable sin? What does it mean to blaspheme against the Spirit? Is this a concern in the church today?

three

Being Spirit, Being Spiritual

God created human beings with bodies. Our embodiment is not an accident or a problem. It is God's good intention for us that we should be the sorts of creatures we are, creatures who are both physical and spiritual, creatures for whom the bodily life is the life in which we do what we were made to do. We relate to God as embodied creatures, and God saves us as such. At the same time, God made us spiritual creatures. The language we use for this reality is trickier, in some ways, than language about bodies. Bodies, in their materiality, are solid facts we can name. Our spirituality is more difficult to describe, but most Christians speak of the human soul when trying to describe the fact that God made us as spiritual creatures, creatures who reflect his image and are able to have genuine relationships with him.

As spiritual-physical creatures, embodied souls or ensouled bodies, we are sometimes surprised to find ourselves in relationship with a God who is so very different from us. God is not just more than us or bigger than us. God is different from us in quality or kind. God is God, and we are not. The affirmation that God *is* Spirit points to the essential difference between God and us. We have ways to acknowledge the holy mystery and majesty of God's otherness. We use reverent language like "holy mystery and majesty" and technical terms such as *immutability, simplicity, transcendence,* and *ineffability.* The basic terms *spirit* and *spiritual* are probably the most common words Christians use to point to the wondrous difference between God and us. John Wesley, in a sermon on the unity of the divine being, highlights just this point: "This God is a spirit; not having such a body, such parts, or passions as men have. It was the opinion both of the ancient Jews and the ancient Christians that he alone is a pure spirit, totally separate from all matter."[1] Paul evokes the same feeling with his "the Lord is Spirit," and he also points to the marvelous relationship that we have with the transcendent, holy God who is Spirit, a relationship in which we are drawn into God's own freedom and are freed from sin, fear, and death.

Augustine's Quandary

The young Augustine of Hippo, who would become one of the most influential Christian thinkers of all time, struggled with the idea of God's spiritual nature. This intellectual difficulty was an obstacle to his full embrace of the Christian faith. Looking back over his life in his autobiographical *Confessions*, he recalls that it once seemed

1. J. Wesley, "Unity of the Divine Being," 533.

monstrous to him to imagine that God could be everywhere. This was because, as a physical creature, he could only imagine physical things. He could only imagine that God must be a bit like us, and he kept supposing that God must be some kind of strange diffuse substance, spread over everything.[2] This false god would be bigger than us, yes, but would not be different from us in kind. Looking back, Augustine recalls how he did not know "that God is spirit, not a being with limbs stretching far and wide, and having a certain size."[3] Here, interaction with the Christian teacher Ambrose and with Platonic philosophy finally helped him imagine spiritual reality, to accept in some way the mysterious difference between God and us. Augustine recounts:

> Although I had not even a faint or shadowy notion of what a spiritual substance could be like, I was filled with joy, albeit a shamefaced joy, at the discovery that what I had barked against for so many years was not the Catholic faith but the figments of a carnal imagination. . . . O God, most high, most deep, and yet nearer than all else, most hidden yet intimately present, you are not framed of greater and lesser limbs; you are everywhere, whole and entire in every place, but confined to none. In no sense is our bodily form to be attributed to you, yet you have made us in your own image. . . . I rejoiced to find that . . . that Church within which I had been signed with Christ's name in my infancy, did not entertain infantile nonsense or include in her sound teaching any belief that would seem to confine you, the creator of all things, in any

2. Augustine, *Confessions*, 6.3.4 (Boulding, 100).
3. Ibid., 3.7.12 (Boulding, 84).

> place however vast and spacious, in any place that would hem you in on every side after the manner of human bodies.[4]

All of this suggests that the word *spirit*, even without the capital letter we use for the Third Person of the Trinity, can be confusing. Various uses of the word *spiritual* only add to the problem. In contemporary life, the language of "spirituality" is employed in incredibly diffuse, obtuse, and generic ways. Some are drawn to "gnostic" ideas that would find spirituality in escape from the body. Others want to be "spiritual but not religious." Eclectic "spiritualities" abound, and these may draw on old pagan traditions and "new age" claims, freely mix Eastern and Western traditions, or plunder bits from several different religions. All of these trends are problematic for Christian faith. All work against the sweet testimony of the Holy Spirit, both in Scripture and in Christian life, a testimony that is concrete, specific, and that matters to us as embodied creatures in distinctly Christian ways. Here, we will look briefly at several ways in which the idea and practice of spirituality goes wrong in our world, and we will consider correctives that come from the doctrine of pneumatology.

Gnostic "Spirituality"

Gnostic pseudo-spirituality has a long history as a distortion of Christian faith. The word *Gnostic* comes from the Greek *gnosis*, meaning "knowledge," and ancient Gnostics claimed to have access to special, secret knowledge that

4. Ibid., 6.4–5 (Boulding, 139–40).

was the key to salvation.[5] Gnostic sects, representing a varied mix of groups active during the first centuries of the church, shared in common a belief that spirituality is opposed to physicality. Gnosticism contained a harsh dualism, an assumption that all that exists must be divided into two categories: good and bad, light and dark, spiritual and physical. This meant that anything associated with physicality or with bodies was seen, in Gnostic systems, as antithetical to spirituality. Bodies were believed to be unimportant for the spiritual life, and bodies could become prisons to be escaped or so trivial that matters of bodily life—sexuality or food, for example—were irrelevant to morality.

Augustine spent some time as a follower of a Gnostic group called the Manichaeans; they operated out of the Gnostic dualism that pitted materiality against spirituality, and, in their system, disdain for bodies translated into "spiritual" practices meant to free the spiritual from the world of supposedly crass materiality.[6] This meant that Manichaeans tried not to conceive children lest more bits of spiritual light be trapped in the bodies of screaming human infants, and so the group practiced contraception. The older Augustine, looking back, insisted against Manichaean teaching that married sexuality is good and that babies—and their bodies—are good. (For Augustine, this meant rejecting birth control, and his position continues to underlie Catholic teaching on this matter today. Most Protestant traditions would agree with Augustine that sexuality and babies are good, but affirm that the

5. For an overview of Gnosticism, see Rudolph, *Gnosis*.

6. On Manichaean belief and practice, see BeDuhn, *Manichaean Body: In Discipline and Ritual*.

goodness of sex and babies can be upheld alongside the wise use of contraception.) The Manichaeans also engaged in rigorous ascetic practices meant to subdue the body and its evils.

The Christian Augustine recalled his affiliation with the Manichaeans with disgust. He had come to see bodies as good, created by God and intended for redemption in the resurrection. This affirmation of the goodness of bodies and materiality is reflected in the consistent witness of Scripture and the great consensus of Christian teaching. Because God is the creator of all things, material and spiritual, all those created things are good. Because God has redemptive intentions for all of creation, material and spiritual, Christians believe in hope that all will be redeemed in the new creation.

This does not mean that we never have problems with our bodies or with the material world. Bodies are certainly created good, but they, like all of creation, are groaning under the condition of sin. The mature Augustine taught that our problem is not that we have bodies;[7] rather, our problem is sin. Certainly bodies are fallen, and we face that reality in very tangible ways when we deal with cancer or injury or, in Augustine's case, lust. Again, though, the problem is not that we have bodies but that we, body and soul, are sinners in a sinful world. This is not meant to imply that cancer, bodily injury, or even lust is the punishment for the personal, individual sin of the one whose body is affected. The fallen state of the world is both individual and communal, and all of us, both in innocence and guilt, feel the effects of sin in

---

7. See my *Marks of His Wounds: Gender Politics and Bodily Resurrection*.

both body and soul. Certainly bodies are fallen, but the spiritual aspects of human existence are fallen as well. Body and soul, though, we have hope in Christ: hope that God—who made us spiritual creatures able to be in personal relationship with him—will sanctify us, body and soul.

Gnostic spiritualities, which are not confined to the ancient world and continue to pop up in the contemporary church, tell the lie that the body is opposed to the spiritual life. They tell the lie that truly spiritual people disdain or try to escape from the bodily life; or they tell the opposite lie that it does not matter what spiritual people do with their bodies. Against this, the truth of Scripture testifies that

1. All things, material and spiritual, heaven and earth, body and soul, are good because created by a good God.

2. God created human beings as embodied creatures, both spiritual and physical, and God loves us as such.

3. All of those things named in point one are subject to sin. The spiritual aspect of human life is no less fallen than is the physical.

4. Jesus Christ, who is truly God, is the example of the spiritual life, and he came to dwell among us in this world, body and soul, in the incarnation.

5. God's redemptive work in human lives is for every aspect of those lives, both spiritual and physical, and God works, through the power of the Holy Spirit, to transform us, body and soul, into the loving image of Christ.

6. Final redemption includes bodies and souls. We hope for the final resurrection, in which we, like the risen Christ on Easter, will be transformed, body and soul.

7. The spiritual life is the life of body and soul under the direction of the Holy Spirit. Christian spirituality is physical and spiritual, embodied and ensouled, contemplative and active, messy and transformative.

Human spirituality, under the tender guidance of the Holy Spirit, is something altogether different from the Gnostic lie. It embraces the goods of this life even while recognizing the terrible struggles we face under the condition of sin. It has nothing at all to do with a rejection of bodies. It has everything to do with the Holy Spirit, who is God, the Lord, the giver of life. Gustavo Gutiérrez, known as the father of liberation theology, puts it beautifully:

> Spirituality, in the strict and profound sense of the word, is the dominion of the Spirit. . . . A spirituality is a concrete manner, inspired by the Spirit, of living the Gospel; it is a definite way of living "before the Lord," in solidarity with all human beings, "with the Lord," and before human beings. It arises from an intense spiritual experience, which is later explicated and witnessed to.[8]

Spiritual and Religious

Given that Gnosticism is a lie, it is problematic to claim to be "spiritual but not religious." Generally, this expression

8. Gutiérrez, *Theology of Liberation*, 117.

Being Spirit, Being Spiritual

signals something like the Gnostic dualism that would divide spirituality from the stuff of the material world. The claim to be "spiritual but not religious" tends to rest on the assumption that spirituality concerns the inner person—the heart, the mind, the soul, the emotions, or the intentions—and so does not concern bodily things. Because this version of spirituality is believed to be something interior, it is also considered private and not something to be inflicted on the outside world, in which toleration is the ultimate virtue. The same sentiment, that of being "spiritual but not religious," tends to equate religion with dead forms, meaningless rituals, and dogmatic beliefs. This brand of popular spirituality will not do for Christians, whose spirituality must be about life in the Holy Spirit. Because the Holy Spirit, the transcendent God, is intimately involved in creation, because the Holy Spirit works with and in the material world, stuff matters.

This is not to say that the critique of "religion" implied in the idea of being "spiritual but not religious" has no merit at all. A religion of dead forms and meaningless rituals *is* a problem for the Christian spiritual life, that life lived in the Holy Spirit, just as a spirituality of interior feelings is a problem. The Christian spiritual life, following the example of Jesus, is a life in which every aspect of our being becomes one integrated whole. In that integrity—unity and wholeness of body and soul—we are transformed in holiness and enabled to witness to the love of God. If Gnostic spirituality brackets everything material out of the spiritual life, pushing bodies and action and practices to the side, perhaps the dead religiosity that those who would be "spiritual but not religious" tend to disdain brackets the interior out of the religious life, pushing emotions and commitments and contemplation to the side. Neither kind of bracketing is Christian.

In the spiritual life, guided by the Holy Spirit, all is united in an integrated whole: interior and exterior, individual and corporate, soul and body, contemplation and action, commitment and practice, emotion and the day-to-day life of the church. The Christian life must always be spiritual *and* religious in this sense. False spiritualities are revealed as false in the truth of the Holy Spirit, and nominal religiosities are revealed by that same Spirit as the dead things they are. But in no way is it the case that ritual, form, doctrine, corporate worship, sacrament, liturgy, and all the other specific manifestations of religious life in the Christian church must be likewise dead. Not at all. The Holy Spirit, the Spirit of life, gives life to these things and to us, offering us a spiritual integrity like that of Christ.

The Spirit and Bodies

Theologian Eugene Rogers sees, in Scripture, that the Spirit "rests on" bodies. Rogers highlights ways in which the Spirit, "in classical Christian discourse 'pours out on all flesh,'" and he bemoans that "in modern Christian discourse, [the Spirit has] floated free of bodies altogether."[9] Rogers asks a provocative question: "What if the Spirit had grown boring because it no longer had anything to do with the body?"[10] He suggests that neglect of the Spirit may be rooted in this fundamental error, and he insists

9. Rogers, *After the Spirit*, 1.
10. Ibid.

that the Spirit is "immanent in bodily things."[11] Rogers' thesis agrees with my assessment above. Indeed, the Spirit loves bodies and rests upon them.

One of the most marvelous truths of pneumatology is that the Spirit, who is truly God, who is transcendent and glorious and holy and not-like-us, also chooses to dwell within us. The Spirit rests *on* bodies (and this is no small thing), but the Spirit also lives *in* bodies. The crucial biblical passage here is 1 Corinthians 6:

> The body is meant not for fornication but for the Lord, and the Lord for the body. And God raised the Lord and will also raise us by his power. Do you not know that your bodies are members of Christ? Should I therefore take the members of Christ and make them members of a prostitute? Never! Do you not know that whoever is united to a prostitute becomes one body with her? For it is said, "The two shall be one flesh." But anyone united to the Lord becomes one spirit with him. Shun fornication! Every sin that a person commits is outside the body; but the fornicator sins against the body itself. Or do you not know that your body is a temple of the Holy Spirit within you, which you have from God, and that you are not your own? (1 Cor 6:13–19)

Bodily matters—in this case, sex with prostitutes—are spiritually important. One cannot split off body from soul, as though what one does with one's body is insignificant. Spiritual practices in the Wesleyan tradition, embodied practices, acknowledge this reality in that they involve the body. The Wesleyan small group meeting, concern for the poor and hungry, meeting for love feasts or potlucks: all

11. Ibid., 2.

God the Spirit

these are practices in which we are gathered by the Spirit, to whom our bodies matter.

The body is purposeful, goal oriented. The body is *for* the Lord. What is more, the Holy Spirit indwells us so that our bodies become temples. Here, we learn of the miracle that the Spirit—holy and transcendent, utterly different from us—chooses us. The Spirit is with us and loves us and does not disdain us. Poet John Donne relishes just this glorious contradiction:

> Wilt thou love God, as He thee? then digest,
> My soul, this wholesome meditation,
> How God the Spirit, by angels waited on
> In heaven, doth make His Temple in thy breast.[12]

Digest it, indeed: this sweet, strange gift. God the holy, other, transcendent, majestic, magnificent and eternal, takes up residence within us. Here is the gift and power of the Spiritual life, and—Donne is quite right—here is a testimony of God's love for us that ought to provoke us to ardent love for God in return.

Questions for Consideration

1. What are some of the challenges of using the words *Spirit* and *spiritual* in our contemporary culture?
2. What is Gnostic spirituality? Why is it considered a distortion of the Christian faith?
3. What are the key scriptural truths that speak against Gnosticism?

---

12. Donne, "Holy Sonnet 11 (XV)," 116.

Being Spirit, Being Spiritual

4. What does life in the Holy Spirit truly entail with respect to the spiritual life, or the life of Christian discipleship?

5. Why is it important to emphasize how the Spirit not only *rests on* our bodies, but also *lives in* our bodies? What are the moral implications of this claim for Christian practice and conduct, and for ministry?

four

Life in the Spirit

Christian Smith and Melinda Lundquist Denton coined the phrase "Moralistic Therapeutic Deism" to describe "the de facto dominant religion among contemporary teenagers in the United States."[1] Although many teens—and their parents—claim to be Christian, Smith and Lundquist's interviews turned up very little evidence of the concrete beliefs of Christian faith. Instead, they showed a pattern of adhering to a generic faith the authors' characterized as "Moralistic Therapeutic Deism." The "moralism" here is the widespread belief that God wants people to be nice and that "when they die, good people go to heaven."[2] The "therapeutic" aspect refers to a sense that the "central goal of life is to be happy and to feel good about oneself." Finally, the "deism" refers to a sense that God is watching the world from a distance and "does not need to be particularly involved in one's life except when he is needed to resolve a problem." In contrast,

---

1. Smith, "On 'Moralistic Therapeutic Deism,'" 41.
2. Ibid.

Christian spirituality, wedded to the Holy Spirit, is not moralistic, or selfishly therapeutic, or deistic.

Against a moralism that offers only generic virtues—bland goodness and vague niceness—the Holy Spirit grows specific fruit in us. Kindness, among the fruits of the Spirit Paul names in Galatians, is something altogether different from niceness. *Kindness* is a strong word, one that draws on the idea of kinship (kind/kin), of offering to others that warm hospitality that we would offer to our own family. The kinship and the kindness that we know in Scripture are not the weak niceness of American popular spirituality, a smiling exterior that may cover all kinds of nastiness. Human kindness, Christian kindness, as we know it in Scripture is the strong fruit of the Spirit worked in us when we are made "kin," made children of God, and when we learn, from Christ, how members of that family are to be shaped in love. Against a moralism that relies on human effort—teeth gritted as we try desperately to be good—the Holy Spirit works fruit in us by the power of sanctifying grace. Grace is the Christian rebuttal of all moralism. God freely gives grace, and the power by which we, in the spiritual life, begin to be more kind and loving is the power of God, the free gift of grace that allows us to strive against sin and run towards the Lord.

Against a selfish therapeutic spirituality—one that focuses on happiness as defined by the individual—the Holy Spirit offers us the holiness and happiness of the true spiritual life. The problem with a "therapeutic" spirituality is most often found in distorted visions of happiness. The false happiness so often sought in the false spiritual life tends to be individualistic, selfish, and greedy. There

Life in the Spirit

is a wonderful sense in which the Spirit does promise happiness in the spiritual life, for God is our true happiness. There is certainly a sense in which Scripture testifies to our need for "therapy" and healing, but the problems addressed by the therapies of "Moralistic Therapeutic Deism" are generally misdiagnosed. Christian faith names those problems quite specifically. The whole world is groaning under the weight of sin, and sin is an offense against the holiness of God. What we need is not to feel better about ourselves as we are, as creatures stuck in a sinful mire, but to be healed by the gracious power of God, which is made available to us by the cross and resurrection of Christ. What we need is not more toys, more money, or more power, but to find our happiness in God. Augustine expressed this idea in prayer: "the happy life is joy in the truth; and that means joy in you, who are the Truth, O God who shed the light of salvation on my face, my God."[3]

Against the deistic misconception of God—one in which God stands back from it all, the fabled divine watchmaker who leaves the world to run on its own after starting it up—the Holy Spirit indwells us. At this most intimate level, God is with us. God is intimately and tenderly involved with creation and with us, his creatures, at every moment. The Christian spiritual life is founded on the intimate presence of the Holy Spirit in our lives. The Holy Spirit is not aloof, one who might dispense a few rare favors if summoned in times of need. The Holy Spirit is with us every day, at every hour, in our joy and in our sorrow.

3. Augustine, *Confessions*, 23.33 (Boulding, 259).

God the Spirit

Life in the Spirit runs against the grain of popular spiritualities such as Moralistic Therapeutic Deism. Life in the Spirit is a life in which we become the trees who bear the Spirit's good fruit, in which we are given gifts for building up the community, and in which we are sanctified, made loving as we are drawn into the love of the triune God.

Growing Spiritual Fruit

When considering the fruit of the Spirit, those fruits that ripen in us as we live in the Spirit, it is helpful to remember that Paul's enumeration—"love, joy, peace, patience, kindness, generosity [or goodness], faithfulness, gentleness, and self-control" (Gal 5:22–23)—comes in the context of his letter to the Galatians, a letter that is about the grand themes of the gospel. These fruits, the lush bounty of the spiritual life, are gospel fruits. They grow, not by our own desperate effort, but from the good trees that God cultivates through the gospel of Jesus Christ.

The chapter in Galatians that ends with the fruit of the Spirit begins with the glorious freedom that we have in Christ. "For freedom Christ has set us free" (Gal 5:1) is a great call to liberation from the sin and legalism that, outside of Christ, would bind us fast. This stunning line— "for freedom Christ has set us free"—comes in the context of Paul's diatribe against those who would harness new Christian converts to the requirement of circumcision according to Old Testament law. Paul proclaims that we are saved through God's grace alone, rather than as a result of something we have done, or anything we ever could

Life in the Spirit

do. The law cannot make us righteous in God's eyes, and there is nothing in us that can purchase heaven or earn salvation. The good news of the gospel is that, in Christ, we are free from legal burden, and moreover, free from sin and from death.

Even better, the good news of the gospel opens up for us, in Christ, a positive freedom. Through the power of the Holy Spirit, we are freed *for* love and faithfulness and service and holiness. Thus, "do not use your freedom as an opportunity for self-indulgence, but through love, become slaves to one another" (Gal 5:13). Right here in this magnificent riff on Christian freedom, Paul rejoices in how we become, again, slaves. We are to serve one another in love. We are free to care for each other in ways that would not be possible were Christ not victorious over sin. Finally, we are free to bear spiritual fruit. We misunderstand the fruit of the Spirit entirely if we do not recognize that those fruits are gracious gifts, made possible because of what God has done and is doing in our lives. It would make very little sense for Paul to pull away one legal requirement, that of circumcision, only to insist on the far more rigorous requirements that would be involved if we were to treat the fruit of the spirit as legal requirements for salvation. The whole sweep of Galatians reminds us that we can do nothing to earn salvation. Love, joy, and peace are not about earning God's favor. We are enabled to bear these fruits because God has already forgiven our sin and made us part of his new creation. This fruitful feast is itself a gift of grace to which we have no access without God.

God the Spirit

Rejecting Legalism and Antinomianism

The free Christian, in the power of the Holy Spirit, walks a graced road between the perils of legalism and antinomianism. Legalism is the mistake we sometimes call "works righteousness," the belief that we can somehow merit salvation if we do enough, if we obey God's law. Antinomianism is the opposite mistake; Dietrich Bonhoeffer spoke of it in terms of "cheap grace,"[4] the belief that salvation by grace means that we can ignore the law ("anti-" means against, "nomos," the law). The antinomian chooses sin, thereby acting against God's holy will, as though grace were a cover for hedonism, selfishness, and evil. Christ, as the end of the law, is the only one who can fulfill its holy demands, who undoes legalism with all its sad, sweaty, and fruitless attempts to earn salvation. And so we are set free from all our pathetic attempts at self-justification. The empowering Spirit reveals the antinomian option as the lie that it is, and the same Spirit cultivates holy fruit in us, opening the way for the truly free life. This way of describing the Spirit-filled Christian life, against both legalism and antinomianism, is fully characteristic of the preaching of John Wesley, which holds grace together with holiness in the Christian life.

Jesus also used the image of fruit to talk about the Christian life, and his teachings here make sense alongside the message of Galatians. Jesus tells his disciples that they will know false prophets "by their fruits" (Matt 7:16). "Are grapes gathered from thorns, or figs from thistles? In the same way, every good tree bears good fruit, but the

4. Bonhoeffer, *Cost of Discipleship*, 43–56.

Life in the Spirit

bad tree bears bad fruit" (Matt 7:16–17). In the Gospel of John, Jesus says,

> I am the true vine, and my Father is the vinegrower. He removes every branch in me that bears no fruit. Every branch that bears fruit he prunes to make it bear more fruit. You have already been cleansed by the word that I have spoken to you. Abide in me as I abide in you. Just as the branch cannot bear fruit by itself unless it abides in the vine, neither can you unless you abide in me. I am the vine, you are the branches. Those who abide in me and I in them bear much fruit, because apart from me you can do nothing. (John 15:1–5)

We need to read these texts—Galatians 5, Matthew 7, and John 15—together in order to see how fruit grows in the spiritual life. As we have seen, Christian freedom is about grace and holiness. Salvation is a free gift from God, and that gift unites us with Christ and makes us into new creatures, new kinds of trees capable of bearing fruit we would not have been able to produce on our own. To play with the language of Matthew 7, where there used to be thorns and thistles, there are now fig trees and grape vines. If we hope for thistles to produce figs, we are out of luck, but we have, in Christ, changed species, and so we will bear fruits appropriate to what we have become in Christ. What is more, God makes available to us the "means of grace," whereby we receive God's gifts and are enabled to grow in the spiritual life: reading Scripture, receiving communion, accountability with other Christians, and so many more. Order matters here. First, we are redeemed, and only then—helped along the way by God's many means of grace—are we able to bear the fruit of the Spirit.

God the Spirit

The idea of spiritual fruit may seem, in a climate given to Moralistic Therapeutic Deism, like one more way to say "be nice," but biblical teaching about the fruit of the Spirit works against this in every way. Instead of a bland moralism that dilutes strong concepts like love and kindness into watery niceness and deceptive tolerance, we are offered, in life in the Spirit, the wonderful possibility of growing fruitful in a rich variety of ways that reflect the truth about God in the world. Jesus Christ, God incarnate among us, showed us what a life full of ripe spiritual fruit looks like. He lived richly in the fruit of the Spirit, and, following him, we have much to learn about what the fruits look like. Love, for instance, as we learn it from Christ, is rich and wild. Love involves perfect communion with the Father in the Spirit. Love died for us while we were still sinners (Rom 5:8). Love recognizes the stranger at the side of the road as a neighbor, and love does not despise the weak and the lowly. Love, the first of the fruits of the Spirit, has a body in Jesus Christ, and that same love marks us when the Spirit cultivates it in our lives. Just so with the other fruits. We see joy exemplified, specified, and embodied in Jesus Christ, and the Spirit fills us with this joy, not with the selfish pleasure of Moralistic Therapeutic Deism. We see peace, patience, kindness, and all the rest of the fruits exemplified, specified, and embodied in Jesus, and the Spirit grows such fruit in us.

Life in the Spirit

Transformed Body and Soul

The Spirit cultivates good fruit in us day by day, but there is also a sense in which we wait for the fullness of that life. We are already transformed by the Spirit's power, but it is also true that God is not yet finished working this transformation in us. The Spirit's work includes the present life and the life to come, and we saw a preview of what the Spirit will do with us in the life to come when the same Spirit raised Jesus—body and soul—from the dead. So, Paul tells us, "if the Spirit of him who raised Jesus from the dead dwells in you, he who raised Christ from the dead will give life to your mortal bodies also through his Spirit that dwells in you" (Rom 8:11). The Spirit's work in giving life to our bodies begins today and will be finished in the kingdom of God. The Spirit's work of resurrection is to transform us into creatures who, like our risen Lord, live fully in victory over sin and death.

We get a hint of this work in the well-known scene in Ezekiel 37, in which the prophet is brought to the valley full of dry bones and preaches the word from God that we "shall know that I am the Lord, when I open your graves, and bring you up from your graves, O my people. I will put my spirit within you, and you shall live" (Ezek 37:13–14). When Jesus rose from the dead on Easter, we saw the firstfruits of the Spirit's power of making bones live, and, in Paul's first letter to Corinth, we see the promise that we too will share in a resurrection like Christ's.

Paul is speaking of our own promised resurrection when he says, "What is sown is perishable, what is raised is imperishable. It is sown in dishonor, it is raised in glory. It is sown in weakness, it is raised in power. It is sown a physical body, it is raised a spiritual body. If there is a physical body, there is also a spiritual body" (1 Cor 15:42–44). Paul contrasts the body now—in Greek, the *soma psychikon*—with the resurrection body that will be ours in the kingdom of heaven—the *soma pneumatikon*. The biblical translation I have just quoted calls these the "physical body" and the "spiritual body," but this translation is very misleading. Whether in the present world or in the world to come, the body here is a physical body; that is what the Greek word *soma*, which appears in both phrases, indicates. The distinction between now and the resurrection is not one between materiality and immateriality. Both kinds of bodies are material. Paul's distinction is between two kinds of material bodies: bodies that are guided by our own sinful desires, and bodies that are guided by the Spirit. The *soma psychikon* is under the direction of the selfish human psyche, whereas the *soma pneumatikon* is under the direction of the Holy Spirit. The Christian spiritual life is a life in which we are transformed, body and soul, into the image of the resurrected Christ.

Questions for Consideration

1. What is the fruit of the Spirit? How is such fruit at odds with the kind of generic "Moralistic Therapeutic Deism" that predominates among teenagers in America? Share.
2. What is the Christian retort to moralism, and what is the role of the Holy Spirit in offering us the grace of a true spiritual life?

Life in the Spirit

3. Not only does the Spirit grow fruit in us, but through the power of the Spirit we are freed from sin and freed for love and faithfulness. Share how this is the "good news" of life in the Spirit.

4. Explain how legalism and antinomianism are at odds with life in the Spirit. How did the Apostle Paul and others seek to combat these two poles?

5. What are the "means of grace," and how do they help us Christians grow in grace?

6. What is the relationship between the workings and power of the Spirit and the resurrection of the body? What does the Spirit's work tell us about the future of our bodies?

five

The Spirit and the Wesleyan *Via Salutis*

> Sinners, turn; why will you die?
> God, the Spirit, asks you why;
> God, who all your lives hath strove,
> Woo'd you to embrace his love:
> Will you not the grace receive?
> Will you still refuse to live?
> Why, ye long-sought sinners, why
> Will ye grieve your God, and die?[1]

Charles Wesley's hymn speaks of the Spirit's wooing all of humanity, which animated the great revivals of the eighteenth century. John Wesley understood those revivals as a great and present work of the Holy Spirit, even as a New Pentecost,[2] and the conversion experiences that marked those revivals continue to shape the Wesleyan theological tradition today. Wesley's soteriology—his theology about salvation—was formed in those revivals. The Spirit works powerfully in the entire process of

1. C. Wesley, "Hymn XIV," 85.
2. Hindmarsh, *Evangelical Conversion Narrative*, 102, 118.

salvation, giving the grace without which we would have no hope of salvation and cherishing the integrity of the persons being saved.

Wesleyans and the Way of Salvation

Wesley begins his sermon "The Scripture Way of Salvation" by rejecting mistaken ideas about salvation. Salvation, he preaches,

> is not what is frequently understood by that word, the going to heaven, eternal happiness. . . . It is not a blessing which lies on the other side of death, or (as we usually speak) in the other world. . . . It is not something at a distance: it is a present thing, a blessing which, through the free mercy of God, ye are now in possession of. . . . [T]he salvation which is here spoken of might be extended to the entire work of God, from the first dawning of grace in the soul till it is consummated in glory.[3]

This sermon, a foundational text in the Wesleyan tradition, refers constantly to the work and power of the Holy Spirit in every aspect of salvation. That process includes "what is frequently termed 'natural conscience', but more properly, 'preventing grace'; all the drawings of 'the Father', the desires after God, which, if we yield to them, increase more and more; all that 'light' wherewith the Son of God 'enlighteneth everyone that cometh into the world. . . . [A]ll the convictions which his Spirit, from time to time, works in every child of man."[4] The new birth is the birth

3. J. Wesley, "Scripture Way of Salvation," 372.
4. Ibid., 373.

The Spirit and the Wesleyan Via Salutis

of the Spirit, and "from the time of our being 'born again' the gradual work of sanctification takes place"[5] through the enabling power of the same Spirit. From "the first dawning of grace" through every step on the way of salvation, the Spirit is present and powerful.

The phrase *ordo salutis*—"order of salvation"—is used in Christian theology to describe our efforts to understand the different aspects of God's saving activity in our lives. Scripture speaks of God's saving work in a wealth of ways, and different theological traditions have tried to make sense of these riches. While there is substantial ecumenical consensus about key Christian teachings like the doctrine of the Trinity, the doctrine of salvation is famously—perhaps infamously—less defined in the ecumenical landscape. Various expressions of the "order of salvation" are typical of various traditions, and this ecumenical diversity seems able to exist, if sometimes a bit contentiously, alongside ecumenical unity in understanding salvation as wrought through the grace of God found in the cross and resurrection of Jesus Christ.

John Wesley's understanding of the riches of God's saving activity is better described as a *via salutis*—"way of salvation"—than as an *ordo*. Wesley scholar Randy Maddox explains that the idea of a way of salvation avoids the connotations of the Reformed *ordo* that the different aspects of salvation be construed "as a series of discrete states." It also speaks against the Reformed denial of "the possibility of regression."[6] Wesley, especially in his mature work, lays "much more emphasis on the gradual nature of

---

5. Ibid., 374.
6. See Maddox, *Responsible Grace*, 158.

salvation and the interrelationship of its different facets. On these mature terms, he saw Christian life as a continuing journey into increasing depths of 'grace upon grace.'"[7] Even so, there remains some minimal sense of chronological order in the Wesleyan way of salvation, and the differences between Wesleyan and Reformed theologies matter here. Characteristic tendencies in Wesleyan pneumatology partially account for those Wesleyan-Reformed differences. First, Wesleyan pneumatology tends toward an enormous confidence in the power, presence, and work of the Holy Spirit. Second, Wesleyan soteriology attends to the concrete, cooperative ways in which the Spirit works in human lives. In order to place these claims in the context of Wesleyan and Reformed discussions about salvation, we will have to note some points of agreement and disagreement between the theological traditions.

First, we need to recognize the shared starting point for both Reformed and Wesleyan treatments of salvation. The two traditions agree about the problem that salvation solves. Salvation is *from* something, and Reformed and Wesleyan theologies both follow in the broadly Augustinian and more narrowly Protestant traditions of understanding the human problem in terms of the crippling effects of original sin. God created human beings as good creatures, made in his own image and intended for holy relationships with each other and with God. This holy and happy condition of original righteousness was broken by the fall of all humanity into sin, and the whole human race now lives under the condition of sin. We need salvation, not just because we have sinned as

7. Ibid.

The Spirit and the Wesleyan Via Salutis

individuals, but also because human nature itself is fallen. "No man loves God by nature," preaches Wesley. "To love God! It is far above, out of our sight. We cannot, naturally, attain unto it."[8] Reformed and Wesleyan theologies thus share a diagnosis of the human situation. We are in serious trouble. We are unable to save ourselves. We require healing, and we stand in need of grace. In Wesley's words, "the great Physician of souls applies medicine to heal this sickness; to restore human nature, totally corrupted in all its faculties."[9] When we know the gravity of sin, we are able to know something of the greatness of God's grace. "By nature ye are wholly corrupted; by grace ye shall be wholly renewed."[10]

This understanding of the human situation is not exclusive to the Reformed and Wesleyan communities; it describes a consensus reading of Scripture that dates back at least to Augustine's rejection of the Pelagian heresy, which entertains a false optimism about human nature, teaching that human beings are capable of loving God on our own, without God's gracious help. These same biblical themes were key in the theological debates of the Protestant Reformation, and Protestant identity was defined largely in terms of this rejection of any possibility of works righteousness. Salvation is from God alone, a gift of grace that can never be earned. Here, both the Reformed and Wesleyan traditions stand within the Protestant consensus on salvation. The traditions agree: we need to be rescued by God's freely given grace. In high-

8. J. Wesley, "On Original Sin," 330.
9. J. Wesley, "Scripture Way of Salvation," 332.
10. Ibid., 334.

lighting the truth that salvation is by grace—and not by works—Protestant orders of salvation tend to introduce a pause[11] between justification (God's work of forgiving our sin, by which we are declared righteous in God's eyes) and sanctification (God's work in transforming us into new creatures, making us actually holy). This Protestant pause highlights the gracious truth that justification is *not based on* sanctification. We do not have to perform holiness in order to earn God's forgiveness; indeed, we cannot. This may seem to be taking us far from pneumatology, but we need to understand this shared space before we can see how Wesleyan-Reformed soteriological differences are related, in no small part, to pneumatology.

In the Reformed *ordo,* salvation is based on God's decree. God does not elect one for damnation and another for salvation because they meet (or fail to meet) any requirements that God has for salvation. God's sovereign electing will is the only basis for the work of justification and sanctification that will follow, and, in the Reformed tradition, this "unconditional election" ensures that salvation is by grace and not by works. Wesleyans share the teaching that salvation is a gift, by grace alone, but Wesleyans tend to fear that "unconditional election" underemphasizes the passionate love of God, a love that wishes that all might be saved and that sent the Son as an atoning sacrifice for the "sins of the whole world" (1 John 2:2). Wesleyans read Scripture as testifying that this loving God opens up salvation to all who will turn to him in love, and so the Wesleyan tradition tends to name various events that occur in an individual's relationship with

---

11. Alister McGrath characterizes this Protestant pause in his Iustitia Dei, 212.

God—events such as conviction, contrition, repentance, and coming to saving faith—as happening before (or perhaps simultaneous with) the event of justification. In other words, something happens in the human soul and mind and heart and life that goes along with our being saved. Because of the great freedom of grace, we are empowered to become true participants in the love relationship with God. The Reformed tend to fear that this makes salvation depend on human works—repentance and the like—but Wesley insists that this is not the case because those events were impossible in our natural sinful state. The events that Wesleyans tend to see, in the way of salvation, as preceding the new birth, are *not* works by which we earn salvation. They are gracious and graced ways in which God works *with* human beings in saving us, and they would be impossible without the regenerating presence and power of the Holy Spirit in our lives.

"There are few places," Maddox tells us, "where the typical Reformed *ordo salutis* differs more from Wesley's understanding . . . than the issue of regeneration."[12] For Reformed theology, the "crucial point . . . was that the New Birth must take place before humans can respond to God in any way."[13] The Reformed fear, then, was that the Wesleyan way of salvation underestimated the gravity of human sin and the depth of our need for grace. Wesley is sensitive to these realities, and he too maintains the Protestant "pause" between justification and sanctification.

12. Maddox, *Responsible Grace*, 159.
13. Ibid.

Justification and sanctification though, are not the whole of God's regenerative work. God works to regenerate dead sinners both before justification and after sanctification begins. *Prevenient grace* is the key Wesleyan category here. Prevenient grace is a grace that goes before us, and, on Wesley's reading of Scripture, a grace that is universally available to all people because of what Christ has done. This prevenient grace is precisely a "crucial degree of regeneration prior to the New Birth."[14] Wesley's recognition of the regenerative power of prevenient grace, available to all through the merits of Christ alone, allows him to hold his Protestant assessment of the gravity of original sin together with his teaching, grounded in pneumatology, that repentance comes before the New Birth and that this same repentance is something in which we humans, as creatures in genuine relationship with God, are actual participants. This teaching is not "works righteousness," for it "is only through the benefits of this expression of God's gracious provenience that anyone can turn to God in repentance and receive the more extensive renewal that comes from a restored pardoning relationship with God."[15] We are broken sinners who can do nothing without grace, and, just as true, the power of the Holy Spirit works in and with us to bring us to repentance, justification, and sanctification. One biblical text central to this understanding of prevenient grace comes from John's Gospel: "to all who received him, who believed in his name, he gave power to become children of God, who were born, not of blood or of the will of the flesh or of the will of man, but of God" (John 1:12–13).

14. Ibid.
15. Ibid.

The Spirit and the Wesleyan Via Salutis

Grace Does Not Work by Force

The Wesleyan way of salvation, like the Reformed order, proceeds with the knowledge that nothing is possible for humans bound by sin without God's gracious work in our lives. The Wesleyan way of salvation, unlike the Reformed order, insists that God's regenerating grace is available, not only to the elect, but to all. Prevenient grace—and Wesley discerns this through pneumatological experience—works cooperatively in and with us in opening up the possibilities of conviction, contrition, and repentance. It is through prevenient grace that we are enabled to come freely to saving faith. Nineteenth-century Wesleyan theologian John Miley articulates his opposition to the Reformed "unconditional" elective decree without in any way denying that the "conditions" we bring are themselves gifts of the Spirit. "Whatever may be conditional to regeneration," says Miley, "or whatever must precede or accompany it, still it is efficaciously wrought by the power of the Holy Spirit."[16] Neither of the two sketches below represents the only way to imagine soteriology in that tradition, but these sketches do show key differences between Wesleyan and Reformed soteriologies.

> Reformed *ordo:*
>
> All are dead and powerless in sin, and God's eternal unconditional electing will decrees that some will be saved based on the merits of Christ's work → regeneration enables the elect to receive justification → sanctification begins → glorification

---

16. Miley, "Agency of the Spirit," 208.

Confessing the Triune God

Wesleyan *via:*

> All are dead and powerless in sin, and God's prevenient and regenerating grace is made available to all based on the merits of Christ's work → prevenient grace enables repentance, contrition → justification, a gift of grace → sanctification begins → entire sanctification → glorification

The best of Wesleyan theology recognizes the richness of God's salvific work and that "each stage is premised upon God's justifying grace in Jesus Christ. Through these ministries the Spirit wishes to draw and persuade, not force, the human will; to convince, not coerce, in order to enable the deepest possible experience of God's saving action."[17] And so the Wesleyan tradition has been unafraid of proclaiming the need for human beings to search after, to thirst for, salvation. While it is unfair to suppose that the Reformed tradition suppresses those needs, it is certainly the case that members of the Wesleyan tradition have seen, in the Wesleyan affirmation of human participation in salvation by grace, a place where some of their Calvinist brethren have failed. Historian Bruce Hindmarsh recounts the testimony of the early Wesleyan Thomas Payne, who believed that "Calvinism had led him to irresponsible acquiescence in fate. This even delayed his conversion: 'But I was a strong Calvinist, and that kept me from the blessing a long time, waiting for the irresistible call, and thinking it horrid presumption to venture upon Christ, till God compelled me by His almighty arm.'" Later, though, along with a Wesleyan understanding of salvation, "Joy broke through, and [Payne] narrated this

17. Oden, *Classic Christianity*, 566.

The Spirit and the Wesleyan Via Salutis

as his conversion experience, an experience that involved repudiating fatalism and fortifying his will."[18] My hope is that this sketch of Wesleyan and Reformed agreement and disagreement serves as a backdrop against which we will better understand Wesleyan pneumatology related to salvation summarized under the next heading.

Pneumatological Confidence and Cooperation

Wesley's understanding of salvation is bound together, at every point, with the great work of the Spirit he had witnessed in revival and conversion, and this made him tremendously confident in the Spirit's presence and power in the entire way of salvation. This confidence in the Spirit is one of the most hopeful features of Wesleyan theology, and the church never ceases to be a people who need to live in this confidence, this well-founded pneumatological hope. The Spirit, in whom we put our confidence, is gracious, and offers grace to us in a multitude of ways. The whole biblical call to repent and believe assumes some role for the human being in the process of salvation, and that role is for the human being empowered by grace.

Wesley's experience at Aldersgate, in which his heart was strangely warmed and he felt the confidence of the Spirit that he was truly a child of God, is a paradigm for conversion in which the human being truly experiences the presence and love of God, not through a frenzy of emotion worked up with great effort, but through divine grace. Wesley scholar Albert Outler highlights the graced-ness of what Wesley experienced;

18. Hindmarsh, *Evangelical Conversion Narrative*, 243.

Outler comments that "Wesley understood enough of his tightly reined temperament to add a crucial adverb: a '*strangely* warmed' heart"[19] and that "Methodist sentimentalists have overstressed Wesley's *feelings* (as so often he did himself, but not here). But Aldersgate and its subsequent developments make more sense if the stress falls on the sheer *givenness* of the assurance of *pardon*."[20] Again, the "workings of the Spirit of God are more deeply inward than self-consciousness can reach; it is prevenient and objective, beyond manipulation."[21] The human being's part in salvation fits together with the classic Protestant soteriology of salvation by grace: "The paradox of conviction is this: Those who most truly repent are those most keenly aware of their dependence on the Spirit, knowing that if the Spirit had not drawn them toward the mercy of God, they would never have reversed course on their own."[22]

Grace works in a variety of ways. Justifying grace works our forgiveness. Sanctifying grace makes us holy. Prevenient grace, as we have seen, goes before us in the process of salvation, lifting us up from the depths of sin and enabling a response to convicting grace. One way of distinguishing grace from grace stands out in this Christian vocabulary as a most helpful way of thinking about the Spirit's work in the way of salvation and in our lives—the distinction between operative and cooperative grace.

19. Outler, "Focus on the Holy Spirit," 166.
20. Ibid., 166–67.
21. Ibid., 170.
22. Oden, *Classic Christianity*, 572.

The Spirit and the Wesleyan Via Salutis

The distinction between operative and cooperative grace provides a way to work through some of the questions about agency and power at stake in the gospel claim that salvation is by grace alone. The category "operative grace" names the ways God works *on* us, from outside us, gifting us with something we were powerless to attain. The justifying grace made available to us in the work of Jesus Christ is operative grace because Jesus is the agent, the operator, the one who acts—when we are helpless—for our salvation. He comes to us, from outside us, and offers the healing and forgiveness we so desperately need. But, Wesleyan theology has always recognized, the story does not end there.

The category "cooperative grace" names ways in which God, in addition to working on us, also works *with* us, and this category is especially appropriate for describing the gracious work of the indwelling Holy Spirit in our lives. The characteristic work of the Holy Spirit, as we read about that work in Scripture, is cooperative, and we have no better example than the Spirit's work in the life of Jesus. Jesus, who became fully human for our sakes, lived and worked in cooperation with the Holy Spirit in the way that humans would do, were we free from sin. Rightly, we cannot imagine the relationship between the Spirit and the Son as one of control or one in which the Son must be overpowered in order for God's work to be done. We must imagine the relationship between the Spirit and the Son, and the particular work of the Spirit in the Son's human life, as one in which the Spirit respects and preserves the integrity of the Son's person and of the Son's human nature. "Jesus embodied" says Methodist theologian Geoffrey Wainwright, "not only the divine initiative but also the human response, not only God's grace but also man's freedom. . . . [T]he God who made us without ourselves will not save us without ourselves."[23] When Jesus comes out of the baptismal waters of the Jordan "full of the Holy Spirit" (Luke 4:1), when the Spirit leads him into the wilderness (Luke 4:1), when Jesus casts out demons "by the Spirit of God" (Matt 12:28), the Spirit *must* be working in cooperation with the Son. Any other possibility is unthinkable. And Christians have every reason, again with confidence in the Spirit's presence and power, to believe that the Spirit works in our lives in a way that parallels his work in Jesus' life.

So we see the Spirit at work in the Christian life more generally. Paul's descriptions of the Spirit-filled life also read most naturally as descriptions of a life in which human beings live cooperatively with the Spirit of God. Why else would Paul address Christians as agents, as people who can choose, with and through the power of the Holy Spirit, to live the Spirit-filled life? Agents, not automatons, are enabled through the gracious presence and power of the Spirit to "put to death" every aspect of the sinful life (Rom 8:13). Children, not slaves, are given the power to live as befits the children of the King. The Spirit does not overwhelm or undo us, but the Spirit "helps us in our weakness" (Rom 8:26).

The prayer in Ephesians that God "grant that you may be strengthened in your inner being with power through his Spirit, and that Christ may dwell in your hearts through faith, as you are being rooted and grounded in love" (Eph 3:16–17) makes most sense if the Spirit

23. Wainwright, *Doxology*, 86. Wainwright notes that John Wesley likes to quote this Augustinian phrase.

The Spirit and the Wesleyan Via Salutis

works in and with us, if the Spirit's characteristic work is that of cooperative grace. If it were otherwise, the human "inner being" in need of power here would not need to figure in the text at all. Our appreciation of the Spirit's cooperativity has the effect, not of diminishing our wonder and gratitude concerning the mercies of God, but of increasing them as we acknowledge the love that considers our personhood as something to be tended with integrity, not something to be overthrown. So, as Wainwright puts it, "In the one direction, human freedom is most truly expressed in the service of God; in the other direction (and this is really the primary movement), divine grace is most truly itself when it is enabling human freedom. When God and humanity are thus not conflicting but concurring, any thought of competition between them is out of place."[24] The same powerful divine Spirit who cares for and works with us as human creatures, is the one who "is able to accomplish abundantly far more than all we can ask or imagine" (Eph 3:20). We are not forced in the spiritual life. We are treasured, redeemed, transformed. We are enabled by grace to truly cry out as children of the Father as the Spirit bears "witness with our spirit that we are children of God" (Rom 8:16).

Questions for Consideration

1. How does John and Charles Wesley's understanding of the presence and power of the Holy Spirit affect their way of understanding salvation?

24. Ibid., 83–84.

Confessing the Triune God

2. Explain the differences between "order of salvation" (*ordo salutis*) and "way of salvation" (*via salutis*). In what ways do the Wesleyan and Reformed traditions of the Christian faith differ in their understanding of the presence, power, and work of the Holy Spirit? What do they have in common? What might these differences mean in terms of ministry?

3. What does the notion of a "Protestant pause" suggest in terms of salvation?

4. How do Wesleyans see the preceding events of conviction, contrition, repentance, and coming to faith as the graceful ways of God's saving us? What is the Reformed fear in light of this understanding?

5. What is prevenient grace, and how is it a key Wesleyan category for understanding the relationship of God with us? Put differently, what is the role of the Spirit in bringing us to repentance, justification, and sanctification?

6. How does the drawing of distinctions between Reformed and Wesleyan views of salvation help clarify the unique understanding of the workings of the Holy Spirit in both traditions? How might these differences contribute to different ways of carrying out ministry?

7. How is the distinction between "operative grace" and "cooperative grace" useful to comprehending the ways in which the Spirit works in us and with us? How is Jesus the example of both operative and cooperative grace?

six

The Sanctifying Spirit Will Perfect Us in Love

> Finish, then, thy new creation;
> Pure and spotless let us be.
> Let us see thy great salvation
> Perfectly restored in thee;
> Changed from glory into glory,
> Till in heaven we take our place,
> Till we cast our crowns before thee,
> Lost in wonder, love, and praise.[1]

This verse of "Love Divine, All Loves Excelling," one of the best-known of Charles Wesley's hymns, expresses the characteristically Wesleyan longing for and confidence in the sanctifying work of the Holy Spirit, work that will "finish" God's "new creation," making us "pure and spotless" and "perfectly" restoring us in love. The sanctifying Spirit leads us into holiness, makes us like Christ, and perfects us in love. In the last chapter, we saw how the Wesleyan and Reformed traditions differ in understanding several aspects of the doctrine of sal-

---

1. C. Wesley, "Love Divine, All Loves Excelling," 384.

vation, but we have not yet explored the most dramatic difference, found in the Wesleyan doctrine of entire sanctification and perfection in love. Wesleyans are wildly optimistic about what God may do with us in this life, and this is only coherent if our hope for holiness rests in the *Holy* Spirit, the third person of the holy Trinity. In the Spirit's sanctifying work, we are drawn into God's holiness, and we are transformed. All Christians believe this, but the Wesleyan tradition is distinctive for its confidence that God's sanctifying grace can accomplish sanctification, not only in heaven but here and now. John Wesley asked those who sought to serve as ordained ministers in the church two key questions about the Spirit's work:

> Are you going on to perfection?
> Do you expect to be made perfect in love in this life?

Trusting in the Spirit's mighty work of sanctifying grace, the candidate answers, "Yes."

The Miracle of Sharing God's Holiness

The word *holiness* has fallen out of our vocabularies, but the truth of God's holiness is central to the biblical witness and to the beauty of the relationship we are called to have with God. To remember that God is holy is to remember that God is set apart, is other, from the world and from us. To invoke God's holiness is to invoke the divine mystery, the truth that God is transcendent, majestic, and mysterious, that God is more than all our categories can suggest. Holiness names the uniqueness and sovereignty of the divine: "There is no Holy One like the Lord, no one besides you" (1 Sam 2:2). Holiness is shown in divine righteousness, the standard of goodness and justice and truthfulness. Isaiah proclaims, "the Lord of hosts is exalted by justice, and the Holy God shows himself holy by righteousness" (Isa 5:16).

And yet, through the whole story of Scripture, God miraculously calls us into the mystery of holiness, including us in God's own righteousness. Moses takes off his shoes on the holy ground around the burning bush, but he is still allowed to approach, to hear the voice of God. The seventh day, the holy Sabbath, is set apart for God, but we are also invited into that Sabbath. God's holy law, the holy sacrifices offered to God, and the holy temple are all testimonies to God's holiness in which the people of God participate. The possibility of human holiness is astounding and real. It is astounding because holiness is God's alone. It is nonetheless real because God graciously gives us ways in which to become holy. The meaning of human holiness is—astonishingly and truly—to be like God. "Sanctify yourselves," the Lord tells his people, "and be holy, for I am holy" (Lev 11:44). If we see holiness as a set of legalistic rules, we are missing the point. Human holiness is seen when we become like God, who is love. Holy human beings, transformed body and soul by the power of the Spirit, receive God's grace by means of practices that involve the body. This may well involve rules, but they will not be stark and senseless ones. One of John Wesley's favorite New Testament moments comes when Peter quotes Leviticus 11:44:

> Therefore prepare your minds for action; discipline yourselves; set all your hope on the grace that Jesus Christ will bring you when he is revealed. Like obedient children, do not be

> conformed to the desires that you formerly had in ignorance. Instead, as he who called you is holy, be holy yourselves in all your conduct; for it is written, "You shall be holy, for I am holy." (1 Pet 1:13–16)

Human holiness is truly a gift of grace. Theologian John Webster asks that we allow our thinking about holiness to be shaped by all that we learn about God in Scripture. Holiness is not blind majesty; rather holiness, as Webster puts it, "because it is the holiness of the God and Father of our Lord Jesus Christ now present in the Spirit's power, is pure majesty in relation."[2] Webster explains, "The holiness of God is not to be identified simply as that which distances God from us; rather, God is holy precisely as the one who in majesty and freedom and sovereign power bends down to us in mercy."[3] God's holiness is the love between the Father, Son, and the Holy Spirit witnessed to in Scripture.

Entire Sanctification

In the last chapter, we saw that both the Wesleyan and Reformed traditions make it clear that our being forgiven is not based on our works. Both traditions go on to affirm that those who are justified continue on to be sanctified— made holy by the power of the Holy Spirit. All Christian traditions agree that we must be made holy before we will be fitted to stand in the presence of the Holy God (Heb 12:14), but the Reformed and Wesleyan traditions

---

2. Webster, *Holiness*, 41.
3. Ibid., 45.

The Sanctifying Spirit Will Perfect Us in Love

differ on the degree of sanctification possible in this life. Reformed theology tends to be relatively less optimistic about the Christian life in the here and now, expecting dramatic sanctification only in the next life. The Wesleyan tradition, by contrast, tends to hold to a fierce confidence in what God can and will do with us, even in this life. Neither tradition—and no sound Christian theology—believes that we are unchanged in this life, and neither tradition—again, and no sound theology—believes that salvation is complete in this life. Wesleyan theology is distinct in hoping for entire sanctification, appropriate for this life, in this life: "unlike the theologians of Roman Catholicism and of the continental Reformation, Wesley insisted that entire sanctification can take place in this life, that the purifier of the soul is neither purgatory nor death itself, but none less than the Holy Spirit of God."[4] Wesleyans claim the many biblical promises concerning human holiness, not only for after death, but for the here and now. The commands are "not given to the dead, but to the living,"[5] and present tense holiness is clearly expressed in biblical texts such as Titus 2:11–14:

> For the grace of God has appeared, bringing salvation to all, training us to renounce impiety and worldly passions, and in the present age to live lives that are self-controlled, upright, and godly, while we wait for the blessed hope and the manifestation of the glory of our great God and Savior, Jesus Christ. He it is who gave himself for us that he might redeem us from all iniquity and purify for himself a people of his own who are zealous for good deeds.

4. Collins, *Scripture Way of Salvation*, 177.
5. J. Wesley, "Biblical Promises of Perfection," 169.

God the Spirit

It would be hard to find a sharper text about present tense holiness than 1 John 4:17: "Love has been perfected among us in this: that we may have boldness on the day of judgment, because as he is, so are we in this world." Wesleyan thought is characterized by this confidence that the sanctifying power of the Holy Spirit is capable of truly transforming us and making us perfect in love.

The "sum of Christian perfection," said John Wesley, "is all comprised in that one word, Love."[6] The beauty of the doctrine of entire sanctification lies in the confidence in grace and the hope for real holiness that it entails. Several passages of Scripture bear repeating here. Paul prays, "May the God of peace himself sanctify you entirely; and may your spirit and soul and body be kept sound and blameless at the coming of our Lord Jesus Christ. The one who calls you is faithful, and he will do this" (1 Thess 5:23–24). One of the senses in which sanctification is "entire" is that the Spirit purifies and empowers every aspect of human existence, "spirit and soul and body." Wesley is well known for insisting that holiness is not just about the exterior, not just about appearing holy. It extends to the heart. After Jesus preaches his radical call to share in the love of God by loving our enemies, he charges us to "be perfect, therefore, as your heavenly Father is perfect" (Matt 5:48). Perfection, here, is to share in the extraordinary love of God, a love that is radical and all-encompassing, a love, like Christ's, that extends to enemies and outsiders. Another sense in which sanctification is entire, then, is that the Spirit draws us into the love of God for

---

6. J. Wesley, "On Perfection," 275.

the entire world, including every lost sheep, everyone whom the world would despise.

There are many images and biblical motifs that help us imagine the sanctified life. Entire sanctification can be seen in terms of the renewal of the image of God (2 Cor 3), the fullness of the fruits of the Spirit (Gal 5), the new creation (2 Cor 5), having the mind of Christ (2 Cor 2), presenting the self to God as a living sacrifice (Rom 12), salvation from all sin (Col 2), and of loving the Lord with heart, mind, soul, and strength (Mark 12). These themes overlap with one another, showing us that perfection in love is not a legalistic to-do list but a way of heralding the biblical vision of humans transformed to share a holy life with a holy God. John Wesley indicates this comprehensiveness in a letter in which he explains, "I take religion to be, not the bare saying over of so many prayers . . . but a constant ruling habit of soul, a renewal of our minds in the image of God, a recovery of the divine likeness, a still-increasing conformity of heart and life to the pattern of our most holy Redeemer."[7]

A Strange Doctrine

The doctrine of entire sanctification is beautiful, but there is no doubt that it is also one of the strangest of Wesleyan doctrines. Other traditions sometimes worry that Wesleyans are in danger of turning sin into a minor problem. I believe the best way to deal with this ecumenical strangeness is, first, to emphasize the ecumenical features of

7. J. Wesley to Richard Morgan Sr., January 14, 1734, in *The John Wesley Reader on Christian Perfection, 1725–1791*, 38.

God the Spirit

Wesleyan teaching, something that I have done in my explanation of the common Christian hope for holiness and understanding of the need for grace, and second, to acknowledge the doctrine's oddness.

The hope for perfection in love *is* strange for many reasons. It is strange because the Wesleyan use of "perfect" and "entire" here does not carry the usual senses of those words. The strangeness of the doctrine requires that we be quite clear about what is *not* involved in perfection in love. The entirely sanctified child of God still has limits to knowledge, still makes mistakes, still struggles with human weaknesses and infirmities, still knows temptation, and, most importantly, still stands at every moment in need of Christ and dependent on grace. Christian perfection is not a static thing. It continues to grow.

The doctrine is also strange in that it may seem to encourage errors such as spiritual pride, blindness to continuing sin, and legalism. Wesley was familiar with these dangers, and he guarded against them in several ways. First, perfection in love in this life is what John Peters calls "wholly relative" in character:[8]

> Even the attainment of perfect love left broad areas of personal excellence still unrealized. There was an infinite distance between any possible attainment here and now and that "full conformity to the perfect law" which stands as the absolute ideal of the child of God. As over against what remained to be won, present attainment was calculated to prompt penitence rather than pride.... Attainment, moreover, was never to be considered a personal achievement. Perfect love came not by accomplishment but by reception.... The

---

8. Peters, *Christian Perfection and American Methodism*, 187.

The Sanctifying Spirit Will Perfect Us in Love

> whole process from first to last was the work of the Holy Spirit. . . . Moreover, this life of the Spirit was maintained on a moment-by-moment basis . . .[9]

The second corrective to abuse of the doctrine is noted at the end of the quotation above; if we are going to make strong claims about human holiness (and we are!), we will have to make even stronger claims about the graced nature of this holiness, the dependence on the Spirit's power that marks every aspect, every moment, of the Christian life. Here, we see again that the doctrine of perfection must be one of confidence in the Spirit's person and power. As John Wesley counseled in a letter, "what impotence in you can be a bar to the almighty power of God? And what unworthiness can hinder the free love of God? . . . [A]ll the promises lie fair before you. The land flowing with milk and honey, the Canaan of his perfect love, is open. Believe, and enter in!"[10] Perfection in love is not that perfectionism that tries desperately to perfect the self by the self's own power and that defines perfection according to the standards of the world. Perfection in love is a gift in which we participate, by the sanctifying cooperative grace of the Holy Spirit, and which transforms us in a love that challenges all the world's standards.

The process by which the Spirit works in us and with us is one that continues throughout the Christian life. Sanctification begins with the new birth, and it continues through the days, weeks, and years that follow, as we become more and more like Christ. Because fruit grows

---

9. Ibid.

10. J. Wesley to Miss Furly, Newcastle-upon-Tyne, June 14, 1757, in *The John Wesley Reader on Christian Perfection, 1725–1791*, 191.

over time, the biblical image of spiritual fruit is a good one for helping us imagine the continuing process of sanctification. As the apple grows from its tiny, green beginning to its full, ripe goodness, so the fruit of the Spirit grows in the Christian life. The Spirit also transforms us in love as we grow in skill and faithfulness as stewards of the spiritual gifts we receive and as we learn together in community what it means to live a holy life.

Sanctification is certainly a process, but the Wesleyan tradition has long recognized that sanctification may also come in an instant, in a moment in which sanctifying grace works a clear change. Wesley scholar Kenneth Collins sees no conflict between the claim that sanctification can be a process and the claim that it can happen instantaneously. Collins speaks about the gradual process of sanctification as one of "normal spiritual development" and the experience of instantaneous sanctification as one that "highlights the graciousness of God, that it is the Holy Spirit and not men and women, who *makes* the heart entirely holy."[11] To experience entire sanctification is to experience death to sin, to know the transforming and purifying work of grace. In granting sanctification, the Spirit sets us free for obedience, free to love God and neighbor. Here, the Wesleyan tradition resounds completely with a more ancient and ecumenical voice, that of Basil the Great, who was instrumental in helping the church recognize the divinity of the Spirit:

> Through Him hearts are lifted up, the infirm are held by the hand, and those who progress are brought to perfection. He shines upon those

---

11. Collins, *Scripture Way of Salvation*, 179.

who are cleansed from every spot, and makes them spiritual men through fellowship with Himself. When a sunbeam falls on a transparent substance, the substance itself becomes brilliant, and radiates light from itself. So too Spirit-bearing souls, illumined in Him, finally become spiritual themselves, and their grace is sent forth to others.[12]

Questions for Consideration

1. Wesleyans are wildly optimistic about the work of the Holy Spirit in this life. How is the sanctifying work of the Spirit central to this optimism?
2. Wesley's two questions—are you going on to perfection; do you expect to be made perfect in this life—are still asked of ordained ministers. How might the church pose these questions more broadly—that is, to all who profess to follow Christ?
3. What is the miracle of holiness? What role does the Holy Spirit have in making us holy?
4. Where do the Reformed and Wesleyan traditions disagree about the "degree of sanctification" in this life? What does this disagreement say about the relationship between sin and grace in the Christian life?
5. What is the nature of "entire" sanctification in the Wesleyan tradition? Or, asked differently, what is the "sum of Christian perfection" for John and Charles Wesley?

12. Basil, *On the Holy Spirit*, 44.

God the Spirit

6. What is the danger that is often expressed regarding the Wesleyan doctrine of entire sanctification? Is this danger justified? Why or why not?

7. What makes the Wesleyan emphasis on sanctification so "strange"?

8. How is the Wesleyan doctrine of perfection different from common notions of perfectionism?

seven

Pentecostal Power, Global Revival, Wildness, and Order

Questions about speaking in tongues, also called *glossolalia*, are among the first I get when I teach about pneumatology, but I have waited to address the topic because it is not as central to understanding the doctrine as are the pneumatological basics we have already addressed. Before we can ask about speaking in tongues, we need some understanding of who the Spirit is and how the Spirit works in our lives. This will help us understand special charismatic gifts and the Spirit's descent on the church at Pentecost, which we read of in Acts 2:

> When the day of Pentecost had come, they were all together in one place. And suddenly from heaven there came a sound like the rush of a violent wind, and it filled the entire house where they were sitting. Divided tongues, as of fire, appeared among them, and a tongue rested on each of them. All of them were filled with the

> Holy Spirit and began to speak in other languages, as the Spirit gave them ability. (Acts 2:2–4)

Here is the presence of the Spirit, visible to the church and to the world, in terrifying power. Here is the Spirit's work made accessible to the senses. Here the Spirit is heard, felt, seen. And here, the Spirit works by providing extraordinary gifts. The church speaks in tongues, and the gathered crowd hears "the native language of each" (Acts 2:6).

The wild power of the Spirit's work at Pentecost and subsequently in the church has always been interpreted in at least two ways. This power can be embraced, perhaps even ecstatically, with a deep confidence in the Spirit's work, or this power can be rejected and denied. Both responses have existed in every age and may even coexist in an individual Christian's life. In the Acts account, we read that "all were amazed and perplexed, saying to one another, 'What does this mean?' But others sneered and said, 'They were filled with new wine'" (Acts 2:12). Both responses, openness and derision, can be problematic when pushed to their limits, but the first response—confident and proper embrace of the Spirit's power—is a defining characteristic of the Wesleyan theological tradition and, more, is one of our tradition's deep strengths.

Fearing or Embracing the Spirit

Why, when the Spirit is God, would we fear the work of the Spirit or question the powerful gifts of the Spirit in the life of the church? What obstacles stand in the way of our confident embrace of the Spirit's power? There can be both good and bad reasons for hesitation around the powerful work of the Spirit.

Some Christians fear talk about spiritual gifts because they have encountered people who misuse the Spirit's name, who justify sin by saying that they are working under the guidance of the Spirit. This kind of hesitation is right and proper. Embrace of the Spirit's power does not imply that anything goes. Nor does it mean that anything people call "spiritual" is truly of the Spirit. We have tools for discerning when the Holy Spirit is at work, as we will see briefly now and in more detail in the last chapter of this book. Sometimes, Christians are put off by talk about spiritual gifts because they have encountered church traditions that insist that people cannot belong to Christ if they do not exhibit very specific spiritual gifts, usually the gift of speaking in tongues. Again, I understand this hesitance. The Spirit is not the leader of some exclusive club, one in which only special Christians can gain membership.

So, there are real reasons to exercise caution around wild claims about the Spirit's power, but there are also bad reasons for such caution, especially when that caution is linked to fear and pride. It is very easy to pretend that one has a "good" reason for suspicion about the Spirit when, in truth, that suspicion is rooted in sin. Here, we sometimes fear the Spirit because we are clinging so tightly to our own illusions of self-control. We want to be in charge, and we are put off by anything that might break into our ordered little universes. So, we fear the radical things that the Spirit is apt to do in the world, and we may disguise that fear with high-sounding excuses. We also sometimes fear that embracing the Spirit's power will open us

God the Spirit

up to ridicule, will make us look weak in the eyes of the world, or we may fear being identified with people who are outside our comfort zone. Here racism, sexism, and classism have, both historically and in the contemporary church, played into temptations for those who are not on the margins to hold themselves aloof from the Spirit's power. If we are suspicious of the Spirit because of our suspicions of "those people" over there, people who are different from us, then we need to pray for the Spirit to work in our lives, to open our hearts to all people, people whom the Spirit loves. And this is one of the historical and theological strengths of the Wesleyan tradition. Our embrace of the Spirit has been connected to an embrace of those on the margins.

Like so many things in the Christian life, proper embrace of the Spirit is located between two problematic poles: fearful rejection of the Spirit and uncritical willingness to call spiritual that which is not of the Spirit. Albert Outler, Methodist theologian and John Wesley scholar, describes these two poles; there is "on the one side . . . the tilt toward various sorts of 'domestication' of the Holy Spirit in Holy Church. . . . [A]lways it has tended to link Spirit too closely with the institutional church."[1] Outler names the other pole as "a tendency toward 'enthusiasm,'" and this charge was, in fact, aimed at Wesley and his followers at the beginnings of the Methodist movement. Problematic enthusiasm, according to Outler, is "always aimed at lifting the level of spirituality in the church, but, almost as often, spreading abroad the im-

---

1. Outler, "Focus on the Holy Spirit," 163.

age of a spiritual *elite*."[2] Outler suggests we look to John Wesley as an example of sound navigation between these two unsound possibilities. Further, Outler names the reasons for Wesley's success here as "persistent concern for a *Trinitarian* doctrine of the Holy Spirit,"[3] along with "habituated awareness of the Holy Spirit as the Giver of all Grace"[4] and a focus on the "internal witness of the Holy Spirit."[5]

Charismatic Gifts

It is easy enough to suggest that we should embrace the Spirit's power without commenting on specific questions faced within the church. When thinking about Pentecost and the Spirit's power, the question of post-Pentecost Christians speaking in tongues has been the source of a fair amount of confusion. Are the special gifts of the Spirit, sometimes called "charismatic gifts," available to Christians in all ages?

Paul addresses these questions in 1 Corinthians, and he makes it clear that the Holy Spirit and Jesus Christ can never be in conflict with one another: "no one speaking by the Spirit of God ever says 'Let Jesus be cursed!' and no one can say 'Jesus is Lord' except by the Holy Spirit" (1 Cor 12:3). Paul goes on to talk about "varieties of gifts" given by the "same Spirit" (12:4), indicating that a diversity of spiritual gifts is to be found among the people of

2. Ibid., 164.
3. Ibid.
4. Ibid., 165.
5. Ibid., 166.

God and that all these gifts, in the unity of the Spirit, are meant "for the common good" (12:7). This is the context for Paul's famous illustration of the church as one body in which there are many different parts, all of which need one another. The gift of tongues is one among many possible gifts of the Spirit but is not to be demanded of all Christians. In fact, Paul relativizes the gift of tongues, putting it under the gift of prophecy, which builds up and encourages the whole church (1 Cor 14:1–6). Paul also advises that eagerness for spiritual gifts should be to "strive to excel in them for building up the church" (1 Cor 14:12), and he counsels that spiritual gifts should be directed toward witnessing to outsiders, so that they may learn the good news of Jesus Christ. While Pentecostal Christianity, which normally expects a second baptism of the Spirit to be manifest in speaking of tongues, is a member of the Wesleyan family, most of that Wesleyan family believes, instead, that we receive the fullness of the Spirit with justification, with no need to wait for a second, special work of grace.[6] Tongues, then, are a possible gift of the Spirit, but not a necessary one.

Against strong forms of "cessationism"—theologies that insist that special charismatic gifts ended in the New Testament age—the Wesleyan tradition has affirmed that special gifts of the Spirit can be and are bestowed in every age. The center of that tradition, though, in consensus with the broader church's reading of Paul above, asks for discernment when talking about gifts of the Spirit and refuses to create a spiritual elite, a special caste of Christians with charismatic gifts. As noted above, Wesley and his

---

6. See Brand, *Perspectives on Spirit Baptism*.

Pentecostal Power, Global Revival, Wildness, and Order

followers were often accused of "enthusiasm," and Wesley denied the accusations even as he embraced spiritual experience. Wesley was enthusiastic about the work of the Spirit in the life of the church, but he also defended his movement against those who accused it of excess.

On Peter's calling the people to "repent, and be baptized every one of you in the name of Jesus Christ so that your sins may be forgiven; and you will receive the gift of the Holy Spirit" (Acts 2:38), Wesley notes that this gift of the Spirit is not "the power of speaking with tongues; for the promise of this was not given to all that were afar off, in distant ages and nations; but rather the constant fruits of faith, even righteousness, and peace, and joy in the Holy Ghost."[7] This comment does not deny that Christians may receive the gift of tongues, but it does deny that all Christians must do so. In his sermon "The More Excellent Way," Wesley begins with an extraordinary defense of the special gifts of the Spirit. He calls the idea that such gifts ended with the early church "a miserable mistake."[8] Wesley attributes any waning of spiritual gifts to a watered-down Christianity, connecting it to "that fatal period when the Emperor Constantine called himself a Christian, and from a vain imagination of promoting the Christian cause thereby heaped riches, and power, and honour upon the Christians in general; but in particular upon the Christian clergy."[9] Wesley's age, like our own, was one that denied the miraculous,[10] but

7. J. Wesley, *Explanatory Notes upon the New Testament*, Act 2:38.

8. J. Wesley, "More Excellent Way," 512.

9. Ibid.

10. For this argument, see Barbeau, "John Wesley and the Early Church."

God the Spirit

Wesley points to human sin, greed, lust for power, and collusion between the church and the empire as causes behind the drying up of spiritual gifts, and he says this is a case in which "'the love of many'—almost of all Christians, so called—was 'waxed cold.' . . . This was the real cause why the extraordinary gifts of the Holy Ghost were no longer to be found in the Christian church—because the Christians were turned heathens again, and had only a dead form left."[11] Clearly, Wesley affirms the extraordinary work of the Spirit in the life of the church. It is not surprising that twentieth-century Pentecostalism and contemporary charismatic Christianity are children of the Wesleyan family. Both the members of more mainstream Wesleyan churches and charismatic Christians often do not recognize the theological connections between their traditions, but I believe that both sorts of churches will be enriched if we do so.

We can summarize a Wesleyan approach to charismatic gifts in six points:

1. We ought to stand open to and hungry for the Spirit's power in our churches and in our lives. If we are closed to the Spirit, something has gone seriously wrong.

2. We can embrace the characteristic pneumatological confidence of our tradition.

3. We must reject a "cessationist" theology, which would confine the Spirit's mighty works to the past.

4. Churches that tend to practice less charismatic forms of worship should not disdain those churches

---

11. J. Wesley, "More Excellent Way," 512.

that do, and churches that focus on charismatic gifts should recognize the authenticity of churches that do not. Both ends of the tradition would be enriched by asking the question, what are we missing?

5. The Spirit does not make claims or give gifts that contradict the Scriptures. Neither does the work of the Spirit contradict the Father or the Son.
6. The gifts of the Spirit build up the church and empower the sharing of the gospel with the world, but this should not be used as a utilitarian test of such gifts, which are also about the intimacy of God with his people.

Gender, Race, Class, and Global Revival

When Christians are open to the Spirit and take the work of the Holy Spirit seriously, we recognize that the gospel is about God's love for people who are marginalized in a world of sin. Historically, embracing the Spirit also means embracing people who are marginalized, and the Spirit often grants power to those who are powerless: to women in a patriarchal or sexist society, to people of color in a racist world, to the poor in systems that privilege the rich. When, in Acts, the Holy Spirit comes on the church in power, Peter quotes the prophet Joel: "In the last days it will be, God declares, that I will pour out my Spirit upon all flesh, and your sons and your daughters shall prophesy, and your young men shall see visions, and your old men shall dream dreams. Even upon my slaves, both men and women, in those days I will pour out my Spirit; and they shall prophesy" (Acts 2:17–18). The time of the Holy

God the Spirit

Spirit is the time of the "last days." This claim is not about prophecies for the end times. Rather, it points to the church, filled with the Holy Spirit, as a kingdom community. The church, in doctrinal terms, is an eschatological reality. The Spirit loves women and men, poor and rich, black and white and brown, young and old. This pneumatological love challenges our sexism, racism, and elitism. We can find many examples of this in the history of the ecumenical church and of the Wesleyan movement. Historian Douglas Jacobsen narrates one example from the twentieth-century Azusa street revivals: "If the real sign of the baptism of the Spirit was more love for others, the communal manifestation of that love was the ability to care for and respect each other across the lines of race, class, gender, and age that normally separated people."[12] Love, care, and respect also extended to church leadership, and so the leadership of women in the church has been a feature of Wesleyan, Holiness, and Pentecostal movement churches. Jacobsen explains, "All in all, the leaders of the Azusa mission believed that God was unfettered and could freely speak through anyone regardless of age, gender, race, or class. The Azusa revival belonged to God, and no one had the right to silence those through whom God chose to speak."[13] Another example of the Spirit's work for the marginalized may be seen in black church traditions in the United States, in the history of abolitionism and the civil rights movement, and religion scholar Phillip Jenkins says that the "socially liberating effects of evangelical religion should come as no surprise to anyone who has traced the enormous influence of biblically based

12. Jacobsen, *Thinking in the Spirit*, 79.
13. Ibid., 80.

Pentecostal Power, Global Revival, Wildness, and Order

religion throughout African-American history."[14] A third example can be seen in Latin American Pentecostalism, in which "the prominence of female Pentecostals has affected the machismo culture of the traditional military establishment."[15]

The Spirit's work in breaking down walls between people extends around the globe. The church of the Spirit and the work of the kingdom transcend national, linguistic, and ethnic boundaries. God is the God of all peoples and all nations, and the Spirit loves those people and nations, uniting us as one while also loving and preserving our diversity. John Wesley, in his notes on the New Testament, sees this dynamic in the Pentecost account: "this family praising God together, with the tongues of all the world, was an earnest that the whole world should in due time praise God in their various tongues."[16] The rapid growth of Christianity around the globe is one of the most remarkable religious and sociological trends of our time, and much of this Christianity is connected—theologically, historically, or spiritually—to the Wesleyan movement's confident pneumatology. Spirit-centered Christianity is growing exponentially in Asia, Africa, and Latin America.[17] The burgeoning scholarship on global Christianity points to these connections. Historian David Hempton says that the "next Christendom, already under construction in the global south, would not look

---

14. Jenkins, *New Faces of Christianity*, 13.

15. Sanneh, *Disciples of All Nations*, 275–76.

16. J. Wesley, *Explanatory Notes on the New Testament*, Acts 2:4.

17. Anderson, *Introduction to Petecostalism*; Jenkins, *New Faces of Christianity*, 12.

the same if Methodism had never existed."[18] Theologian Lamin Sanneh comments on the strength of charismatic Christianity in the growth of world Christianity: "Charismatic Christianity has been the driving engine of the Third Awakening, and it is largely responsible for the dramatic shift [away from Europe and the United States] in the religion's center of gravity."[19]

I want to close this chapter with a long quotation from Harvey Cox, in which he reflects on the connections between Spirit-centered Christianity and the disempowered:

> For pentecostals, the crux of this renewed debate between the primacy of belief systems and that of personal experience may lie in precisely that feature of their life which has sometimes brought upon them the most reproach and caused them the most embarrassment: ecstatic worship—which I believe is a kind of populist mysticism. What pentecostals call "speaking in tongues," or "praying in the Spirit," has appeared in history before, and it is always a sure sign that the available religious idiom has become inadequate. Glossolalia is a mystical-experiential protest against an existing religious idiom that has turned stagnant or been corrupted. But glossolalia does not occur in a vacuum. It almost always takes place among people who are themselves culturally displaced, and often politically or socially disinherited as well. It is a form of cultural subversion, a liberating energy that frees people to praise God in a language of the Spirit that is not controlled by dominant modes of religious

---

18. Hempton, *Methodism*, 209.
19. Sanneh, *Disciples of All Nations*, 275.

discourse. Furthermore, glossolalia helps to create a new religious subculture, one that in turn amplifies and affirms personal experience. There is one thing the critics of experience-based theologies overlook when they claim that culture and language always precede and shape experience. They overlook pain.[20]

The Wesleyan theological tradition is a tradition of the Spirit, one in which we must be open to the Spirit's mighty and powerful work in our lives and our churches.

Questions for Consideration

1. What have been the two typical responses to the Spirit's work at Pentecost?
2. What are some of the "hesitations" or "obstacles" that may stand in the way of our embrace of the Spirit's work?
3. What is stated as one of the primary theological strengths of the Wesleyan tradition when it comes to the workings of the Holy Spirit?
4. What are the two problematic "poles" to navigate when speaking about the role of the Holy Spirit?
5. What are some of the gifts of the Spirit? What dangers may accompany such gifts in the life of the church?
6. What was John Wesley's concern regarding the "drying up" of spiritual gifts in the church? What did such "drying up" portend?

20. Cox, *Fire from Heaven*, 315.

God the Spirit

7. How might we summarize John Wesley's approach to charismatic gifts? Do you find this approach helpful today?

8. What are some ramifications of the Spirit-centered Christianity that is growing in the global south, and what is its relationship to a Wesleyan view of the Spirit?

9. What is the connection between the Spirit and those who live on the margins of society? Why is this connection so strongly emphasized in Wesleyan Christianity? What are the implications for mission in our churches today?

eight

Inspiration, Illumination, and the Spirit in the Church

How can I presume to write a book about the Holy Spirit without quoting huge chunks from the book of Acts? In this book—found in the New Testament right after the four gospel accounts of Jesus' life, death, and resurrection—we read the story of the Spirit's work in the church. It is a tremendous, fearsome, and astounding story. In Acts, God's people are repeatedly filled by the Spirit, prodded by the Spirit, or enabled to speak with the Spirit's words. New Christian converts receive the Spirit. And the Spirit does remarkable things: surprising Peter by including the Gentiles without requiring circumcision, resting on believers with tongues of fire, turning notorious sinners into followers of Christ, strengthening disciples for martyrdom, provoking missionary journeys, working even in the midst of shipwrecks and in spite of prison walls, making it clear that the Spirit cannot be bought or deceived, and so much more. All along the way, the Spirit bears witness to Jesus Christ; all along the way, the Spirit creates and gives power to a community that embodies, in the summary of New Testament scholar Kavin Rowe, "an alternative total way of life—a comprehensive pattern of being—one that runs counter to the life patterns of the Graeco-Roman world."[1] That same Spirit-led and Scripture-shaped community, the church in our own time, also runs counter to the patterns of our contemporary world.

In reading Acts, we, as God's people, learn what it means to live in the age of the Spirit, in the days and years between Jesus' ascension to the Father and the time when he will come again in glory. This is no easy task, and frankly, many Christians might rather live in some other age. Would it be easier, we cannot help thinking, if we could just see Jesus face to face? If we were not stuck in this strange era in which God sometimes seems so absent? And yet, in the book of Acts, we learn about the Spirit-filled gifts and graces of *this* time. We learn to live in the great goodness of the presence and power of the Spirit. We learn to give thanks for and draw strength from Scripture and the church as the Word and the people of the Spirit. In this chapter, we will examine salvation history in the light of pneumatology, paying attention to what it means to live with the Spirit, under the Spirit's care, a people called out as the church of Jesus Christ and gifted with God's inspired Word.

---

1. Rowe, *World Upside Down*, 4.

Inspiration, Illumination, and the Spirit in the Church

The Spirit in Salvation History

In the church today, some believers feel strongly that we stand in the same age as did the church in Acts. Like Lydia, Peter, Priscilla, and Paul, we live and work in the time between Jesus' first and second comings. It is in this time that we, like the Christians in Acts, relate to God and learn the life of faith. Our location in the biblical chronology is sometimes thought of as the age of the Spirit. There is a sense in which this designation is just right and can be life-giving to the people of God in this very age. There is also a sense, though, in which this designation is deeply problematic and, if misunderstood, may be harmful to the life of the church. I want to focus first on the positive sense in which we dwell, right now, in the age of Spirit. When we have understood this, we will be in a better position to understand the dangers of supposing that the Spirit's work is limited to only one age. The key New Testament events follow in chronological order:

1. Jesus of Nazareth is born, lives, and dies. He is conceived by the power of the Spirit, baptized by and filled with the Spirit in his ministry, and goes to the cross in unity with the Spirit's power.

2. Jesus, in the power of the Holy Spirit, is raised from the dead.

3. Jesus ascends to the Father.

4. The church receives the Spirit at Pentecost, visibly and powerfully.

5. That same church, created and sustained by the Spirit, lives and works between two realities. On the

God the Spirit

> one hand, we feel Jesus' absence. On the other hand, the Spirit is present with us in power.

6. We look forward to the future, the second coming of Christ, when we will again see him face to face.

What does it mean to be located in our time and place? To work where we work? To long for the visible presence of Christ while also rejoicing in the presence of the Holy Spirit?

To understand the time that we inhabit, we will have to understand our location in the biblical story of salvation. Most Christians have thought about the significance of the incarnation, death, and resurrection of Christ, about the graciousness of a God who would become one of us, die for our sake, and be raised from the dead, victorious over sin and death. Fewer Christians, in my experience, have thought about the ascension of Christ. What does it mean that the resurrected Jesus—truly God and truly human—did not stay here with us, but instead returned to the Father's side in heaven? Part of what it means is that all the stuff that mattered about God's becoming one of us, dying for us, and being raised from the dead *still* matters. His whole self, divine and human, ascends to the Father, and so Jesus is still God for us, fully God and fully human. His humanity does not end with the ascension. The ascension means that he has become one of us for keeps, that he represents our humanity, right now, today, to the Father.

This list of "goods" about the ascension is good indeed, but we do not always feel it thus. The ascension is a signal to us that Jesus is still one of us, still for us, but it is also the beginning of a different kind of life for his

Inspiration, Illumination, and the Spirit in the Church

disciples, a life in which we do not see him face to face. It is not wrong that we long to do so. I think this is the reason that Jesus is easier for children to think about than is the Spirit. Jesus has hands and feet. Kids can get that. (My son, when he was in kindergarten, was convinced that Jesus lived in our church basement. Embodied people live somewhere, after all.)

It is good and natural that human beings, bodily creatures, should want to see, hear, and touch the one whom we love. Life between the ascension and the second coming of Christ is a life lived with this loss. We, like Thomas, want to touch and see, and being able to do so might well make it easier to confess, as Thomas did, that Jesus is "my Lord and my God" (John 20:28). This loss, though, is not the end of the story. Jesus says to Thomas, "Have you believed because you have seen me? Blessed are those who have not seen and yet have come to believe" (John 20:29). It is significant that, only seven verses before this moment in John's Gospel, the resurrected Jesus breathed on his disciples and "said to them, 'Receive the Holy Spirit'" (John 20:22). To believe when we have not seen is a great good, a good enabled and empowered by the presence of the Spirit in our lives. Peter tells the truth when he says, "Although you have not seen him, you love him; and even though you do not see him now, you believe in him and rejoice with an indescribable and glorious joy" (1 Pet 1:8). We cannot remain like little children, ignoring matters of the Spirit. We learn, in faith, to rejoice in the powerful presence of the Spirit in our lives, a presence that takes its significance partly from Jesus' absence. Jesus describes the goodness of this now, this special time of the Spirit:

God the Spirit

> Nevertheless I tell you the truth: it is to your advantage that I go away, for if I do not go away, the Advocate will not come to you; but if I go, I will send him to you. . . . When the Spirit of truth comes, he will guide you into all the truth; for he will not speak on his own, but will speak whatever he hears, and he will declare to you the things that are to come. He will glorify me, because he will take what is mine and declare it to you. All that the Father has is mine. For this reason I said that he will take what is mine and declare it to you. A little while, and you will no longer see me, and again a little while, and you will see me. (John 16:7, 13–16)

The ascended Jesus' presence with the Father goes together with this special presence of the Advocate—a name for the Spirit—among us. The age of the Spirit is an age of God's own advocacy among us, an age in which we come to understand the things of Jesus better, an age in which the Spirit leads us in truth. The Spirit as Advocate walks alongside us, gives counsel and comfort, and advocates on our behalf.

The Spirit in Every Age

There is, then, a strong sense in which you and I, like the church in Acts, live in a special age of the Spirit, filled with particular gifts and promises; but it would be a mistake, one that has been made too often, to limit the Spirit's work to the present age. The Spirit, as the third person of the Trinity, co-eternal with the Father and the Son, is the God of every age because God is the God of every age. All the work of the triune God, from creation through final

Inspiration, Illumination, and the Spirit in the Church

redemption, is the work of the Holy Spirit together with the Father and the Son. These affirmations work against the mistakes of a heresy called modalism, which would suppose that the Spirit is not truly God but is only a way God acts sometimes. Such a mistake is a sad reduction of who the Spirit is and what the Spirit does among us. The Spirit works in the Old Testament and the New, during the earthly life of Christ and after the ascension, in biblical times and today. The Spirit is not absent before Pentecost.

What, then, is the special quality of the Spirit's work in Acts and in our own age? What does it mean that the Spirit comes in a special way in the events of Pentecost, or when, as we just saw, the resurrected Christ breathes his Spirit on his disciples? Theologian Thomas Oden, in his *Classic Christianity*, gives the section on Pentecost the title "The Spirit No Longer a Transient Visitor"; he draws this language from Augustine.[2] Oden describes the Spirit's descent on the church at Pentecost as a move in which the "one Holy Spirit who before had sporadically called, anointed, and visited chosen vessels, at last came to dwell in and with the faithful community, and in the form of hope with the whole of humanity."[3] Notice that Oden acknowledges that the Spirit has always been God and has always worked among us while at the same time he pays attention to the special presence of the Spirit at Pentecost. "Transient visitor" would not be my first choice of phrase, if transience implies a fickle or flighty Spirit, but I do think Oden's quotation of Augustine here

2. Oden, *Classic Christianity*, 546.
3. Ibid. Here Oden references Heb 8:10 and John 14:15–19.

gets at something of the depth and richness of the Spirit's presence in the time of Acts and in our own time. I like the words Augustine uses in the same passage to contrast permanence with transience—he names the Spirit in the church, after Pentecost, "a perpetual Comforter" and "an eternal inhabitant."[4]

We might also describe the Spirit's work in our age as, in a special way, internal, ecclesial, global, and powerful. While the Spirit of God has always been with God's people, it is only after the ascension that the Spirit indwells us. (One could argue that it makes much more sense to talk about the Spirit living in our hearts than it does to place Jesus there!) While the Spirit of God has always worked among God's people, the Spirit after Pentecost creates and dwells with the church in a special way. While the Spirit of God has always been at work to draw in the nations, it is only in the age of Acts and our own age that the gospel is preached to all the world and the Gentiles are included among God's people. While the Spirit has always been a Spirit of power, the signs and wonders of the present age, which began with Pentecost, have a special significance and visibility as they help us witness to the gospel of Christ. This last point raises one more. Part of the special quality of the Spirit's work in the present age is that, in Acts and now, the Spirit works to bring glory to the historical work of Jesus Christ. The Spirit in the church helps us testify to who Jesus is and what he has done. One of the central tools here, in the Spirit's metaphorical hands, is Holy Scripture. The Old and New Testaments are the book of the Holy Spirit, a book that points us to Christ.

4. Ibid.

The Spirit and Scripture

Two theological categories help us think about the relationship between the Holy Spirit and the Bible: inspiration and illumination. The term *inspiration* refers to the Spirit's work as the author of the Scriptures, a work the Spirit did in and with the human authors of the biblical texts. The term *illumination* signifies the ways in which the Spirit continues to work in and with God's people, as readers of Scripture, to help us understand and be faithful to what we read there. Thus, inspiration names the Spirit's work, in the past, in the writing of the Scriptures. The Spirit is *in* these words, but, as theologian Stanley Grenz reminds us, the "Spirit's work within Scripture did not end in the distant past."[5] Illumination names the Spirit's work, in the present, in helping God's people, both individually and as the church, to read well. The Spirit casts light on (illumines) these words. The Bible, as God's word, is inspired by the Holy Spirit, and the Spirit's illuminating power works with us to help us understand and embody that word. Grenz describes Scripture as "one aspect of the Spirit's mission of creating and sustaining spiritual life. He both authors and speaks through the Bible, which is ultimately the Spirit's book. By means of Scripture he bears witness to Jesus Christ, guides the lives of believers, and exercises authority in the church."[6]

These are strong claims, and we will not have space here to cover the many different ways in which Christians understand illumination and inspiration to work. There are, for example, many different theories about the *means*

---

5. Grenz, *Theology for the Community of God*, 382.
6. Ibid., 379.

of inspiration, and there is no consensus on how exactly inspiration works. The Wesleyan tradition has been content to live with a fair amount of ambiguity here, provided that we begin, following John Wesley, with a high view of Scripture. We can exclude a pair of problematic theories. Given the kind of text that Scripture is and the kind of Spirit we know through Scripture and in our own lives, it cannot be the case that the Spirit inspired the words of the Bible through simple dictation. The Christian Scriptures are a complex collection of texts—called the canon—with human authors from various centuries, locations, and perspectives. When we read the canon, we see that the Spirit, in inspiring the Scriptures, did not erase or smooth over these differences between the human authors of the texts. For instance, the four gospels, all inspired by the one Holy Spirit, reflect the different situations and community needs into which each of their four human authors wrote. The Spirit could have given us one gospel, by dictation, but the Spirit does not work like that. Without understanding the exact means of inspiration, we can exclude wooden theories that would erase the human authors of Scripture.

On the other side of the spectrum, we should also exclude overly loose ideas of what it means to acknowledge the Spirit as the author of these words. In everyday conversation, we may use the word *inspiration* to indicate a very weak connection between two people or ideas, but the Spirit's role as inspirer of Scripture should *not* be understood in such distant terms. While the Spirit has worked in and with the diverse human authors of Scripture, the canonical Scriptures exhibit a deep unity, which is the result of their common author in the Spirit

Inspiration, Illumination, and the Spirit in the Church

and their common testimony to the triune God. What is more, when we recognize the Scriptures as the word of God, we are recognizing a reliable connection between these texts and the God we meet and know there. So, the Spirit's inspiring work is strong and true work. Just as we should not understand inspiration as a mechanistic process, neither should we see it as a loose, distant process. To put the same idea positively, the Spirit's work in inspiring the Scriptures is personal, cooperative, intimate, and particular. Given all that we have discussed in this book so far, none of that should come as a surprise.

A doctrinal standard in the Wesleyan tradition, Article Four of the Confession of Faith provides a basic statement about inspiration and illumination. The claims made there also reflect the broad ecumenical consensus of the church:

> We believe the Holy Bible, Old and New Testaments, reveals the Word of God so far as it is necessary for our salvation. It is to be received through the Holy Spirit as the true rule and guide for faith and practice. Whatever is not revealed in or established by the Holy Scriptures is not to be made an article of faith nor is it to be taught as essential to salvation.

The whole Bible, from Genesis all the way through Revelation, is the Spirit's work. Such ecumenical claims are often grounded in the words of 2 Timothy, in which Paul urges Timothy to live a godly life and to continue in the faith, reminding him "how from childhood you have known the sacred writings that are able to instruct you for salvation through faith in Christ Jesus. All Scripture is inspired by God and is useful for teaching, for reproof, for correction, and for training in righteousness, so that everyone who belongs to God may be proficient, equipped for every good work" (2 Tim 3:15–17). Why is Paul confident that Scripture will be able to work like this in Timothy's life? The answer: Scripture is "totally 'God breathed,' that is, it is completely of divine origin."[7] Gordon Fee identifies Paul's confidence in Scripture here as indicative of his Jewish faith, "which understands the OT as the writings of the 'prophets' (including Moses) and thus links those writings with the Spirit, the acknowledged source of prophetic inspiration."[8] Paul and Timothy, of course, knew the Scriptures as the Jewish Scriptures, which Christians usually call the Old Testament, but, by extension, Christians have always included the New Testament writings in their confidence, recognizing these words, too, as the word of God.

Confidence in Scripture and confidence in the Holy Spirit should go hand and hand, and this has been the characteristic posture of the Wesleyan churches. This double confidence opens for us, as the people of God, the promise and possibility of becoming wise in discernment. Lives lived with that promise and possibility provide a response to objections that too much confidence in the Spirit is liable to become only misplaced confidence in the self. That will be the topic of our last chapter.

---

7. Fee, *God's Empowering Presence*, 793.
8. Ibid., 794.

Inspiration, Illumination, and the Spirit in the Church

Questions for Consideration

1. Why does the book of Acts play such an important role in our understanding of the Holy Spirit? What may be some of the dangers associated with this approach?

2. How does the book of Acts help us make connections between Jesus' ministry and the church's mission in the Spirit?

3. What is the "age of the Spirit"? Is this a helpful term?

4. What is the heresy of modalism, and how is our affirmation of the Trinity important to countering it?

5. In what ways might we describe the Spirit's work in our present age? Share examples.

6. What is inspiration? What is illumination? What is the relationship between the two when studying the Bible? How do we understand the Spirit's work in both inspiration and illumination in the church?

7. How is Article Four of the Confession of Faith a basis for the church's teaching today on the role of the Spirit and the role of the Bible in the life of faith?

nine

Testing the Spirits

Throughout this book, I have tried to encourage us to claim the resources of both Wesleyan and ecumenical pneumatology and to welcome with joy the power and presence of the Spirit in our lives and in our churches. Throughout, I have noted a current of concern that may work against that goal—the concern that we may confuse the Spirit of God with our own desires. Theologian Karl Barth is famous for issuing this warning—that we not equate God with ourselves—in very strong ways. Consider the following quotation, just one of thousands we could pull from Barth's writings, in which he warns the church that we are prone to confuse our sinful desires with what God wants: "When the Gospel is offered to man, and he stretches out his hand to receive it and takes it into his hand, an acute danger arises . . . that he may accept it peacefully and at once make himself its lord and possessor, thus rendering it innocuous."[1] Barth's warning—that we are in "acute danger" of domesticating the gospel and trying to control the work of the Spirit

1. *Church Dogmatics* II.1 26.2, 141.

instead of asking the Spirit to control us—resonated in the twentieth-century church, a siren cry against our own self-delusion.

Barth's warning is both ecumenical and not, both Wesleyan and not. It is shared by the Wesleyan tradition and by the church as a whole inasmuch as it points to a very real risk, one that Christian thinkers have pointed to in various traditions, centuries, and places. The warning, though, if it stops at warning, ceases to be Wesleyan and ecumenical. The broadest consensus of Christian theology is that, yes, we must be careful about self-delusion, but that consensus also moves past this warning to offer positive ways to move forward. We need to take care, but we also have ways to distinguish truth from falsehood and grounds for the hope that, through the power of the Spirit, we may move past delusion and into holiness. The Wesleyan tradition, within this ecumenical consensus, is especially optimistic about this, not because of any false confidence in human beings, but because God the Spirit, in mercy and grace, indwells us and guides us into truth.

The warning and the hope must be held together here. We must take care, lest we claim stupid, selfish, and sinful things in the name of the Spirit. We have means, though, to take such care, means to discern the truth of the Spirit. Discernment is thus a key pneumatological category, and the Christian life is one in which we grow in the ability to discern wisdom and to recognize truth. A passage from the book of 1 John, often turned to by Christians who seek discernment, links together this warning and this hope, and it links them through a Trinitarian theology of the Holy Spirit:

Testing the Spirits

> Beloved, do not believe every spirit, but test the spirits to see whether they are from God; for many false prophets have gone out into the world. By this you know the Spirit of God: every spirit that confesses that Jesus Christ has come in the flesh is from God, and every spirit that does not confess Jesus is not from God. And this is the spirit of the antichrist, of which you have heard that it is coming; and now it is already in the world. (1 John 4:1–3)

We need discernment. We need sound ways in which to distinguish between "every spirit" and the "Spirit of God." And John's test for doing so is christological. Truth is found where Christ is confessed as the one who came in the flesh. John can sound a warning as loud as Barth's—"Many deceivers have gone out into the world" (2 John 1:7)—but John also trusts that Christians, empowered by the Holy Spirit, "have knowledge" (1 John 2:20), and he addresses his letter to people who know the truth.

We have ways of discerning the difference between the promptings of the Spirit and our own (often sinful and selfish) wishes. The theological work in the preceding chapters opens these resources up to us. When we understand something about who the Spirit is and how the Spirit works in the church, we are prepared for discernment. That there is deceit in the world must not impede our confident embrace of God the Spirit, and, when we consider the resources for discernment that are given to us in the Christian life, we will be able to proceed with confidence.

God the Spirit

Not Montanism but Canon

The ancient church encountered these questions in the Montanist controversy, which swirled around the ecstatic prophecies of Montanus, Maximilla, and Prisca. Montanist claims to speak for the Holy Spirit raised questions about authority.[2] Historian Margaret Miles explains that Montanism rejected "the view that the early days of Christianity were normative."[3] What would Christians trust, and what criteria would we use to adjudicate such questions? In rejecting Montanism as a heresy, the church was pointing to the authoritative status of the events of Jesus' life, death, and resurrection recounted in apostolic writings of disciples who were "eyewitnesses" of Jesus' "majesty" (2 Pet 1:16). The rejection of Montanism, for the early church up to the church today, is not a rejection of the power and inspiration of God the Holy Spirit. It is, instead, always a rejection of false claims made in the Spirit's name. The rejection of Montanism is also a critique of the way in which the movement seems to have understood the Spirit's work in human lives. Frances Young points out that the ancient church objected to Montanism, not because Montanists claimed to be full of the Spirit, but because their understanding of being full of the Spirit looked like being possessed. Being inspired by the Spirit should not mean "the evacuation of the prophet's mind, but rather a heightening of the prophet's consciousness. No wonder then that the church used

---

2. Young, *Making of the Creeds*, 50.
3. Miles, *Word Made Flesh*, 49.

Testing the Spirits

against this movement the New Testament warnings to test the spirits and avoid false prophets."[4]

Some historians suggest that Montanism was one catalyst that moved the Christian church toward the "closed" canon of Scripture that we know as the Old and New Testaments. Early Christianity emerged as an outgrowth of Judaism; it was natural that the church would continue to recognize the Jewish Scriptures as sacred. The God we meet in Jesus Christ is the same God we meet in the Old Testament. It was also natural that, given the new things God had done and was doing through Jesus Christ, people who knew him and loved him, whose lives were changed by him, would write about Jesus. Some of these writings would eventually be recognized as Christian Scripture and would become the New Testament. Why, then, could Montanus—and others down through centuries—not add to the authoritative Scriptures? In the communal judgment of the ancient church, new revelations could never have the same authoritative status as the books of the Old and New Testament canon. It made sense to the ancient church—as it does to most Christians in the present day—to grant special authority to the events and writings that came from Jesus' own time. Writings from apostles—those who knew Jesus in person and could give reliable testimony—were thus received as authoritative. The canon of Scriptures is a "closed" canon, meaning it is not open to additions from Montanus or from me, because the Spirit led the church to recognize these writings, and not others, as true testimonies of the faith.

4. Young, *Making of the Creeds*, 51.

God the Spirit

We have already thought about the Spirit as the author of Scripture, but it is also important to see the Spirit's work in superintending the process of canonization. The fact that Christians receive the Scriptures as a collection of texts, written by multiple human authors from many centuries and communities, is a testimony to the way in which the Spirit chooses to work among us. Some people suggest that the process of canonization shows that Scripture is not authoritative. This argument assumes that because human beings authored and, later, assembled the canon, these books are not in fact the word of God. This position is insensible to the Spirit's characteristic ways of working in the world and with human beings. In a similar vein, some would suggest that rejecting Montanism and any postcanonical "revelation" is simply a human power play, an imperialistic attempt to shut down dissenting voices. Again, this argument strikes me as remarkably numb to the Spirit's ways of working. The Spirit is the Spirit of truth, and it should not surprise us that the Spirit separates truth from falsehood. The Spirit is the Spirit of Jesus Christ, and it should not surprise us that the Spirit agrees with and testifies to Jesus. Christian theology does not reject people who claim to know the power of the Holy Spirit working in their lives and even revealing truth to them, but Christian theology will always insist that such testimonies require discernment. Wise discernment recognizes the compelling truth and beauty of the gospel, the centrality of Jesus' life, death, and resurrection, and the work of the Holy Spirit as the author of Scripture. God is true, and God is trustworthy. God does not engage in self-contradiction, and so we can be confident that the same Spirit who inspired the Scriptures and shepherded the process of canonization will, when working in our lives today, do work that is consistent with the Scriptures. The Bible, inspired by God the Spirit, is the primary authority for Christian faith and life and the key to spiritual discernment.

Quadrilaterals and Inner Witnesses

Many Wesleyan Christians are familiar with the idea of the Wesleyan Quadrilateral—the idea that when we are seeking theological discernment, we turn to four sources: Scripture, tradition, reason, and experience. It is common to talk about the four sides of the quadrilateral as if each were an independent authority, like four spokespeople who might sit at the table with us as we seek God's face. This is not—for biblical, historical, and practical reasons—a helpful way of thinking about theological decision-making. If we treat the four sides of the quadrilateral as equal authorities in a quasi-democratic process, then we will be more susceptible than ever before to that which Barth warned us of—the confusion of our sinful selves with the will of God. Scripture sounds this warning, too, reminding us that our best efforts to gain knowledge are limited by sin and finitude. Blessedly, God speaks to us through the word, gifting us with inspired Scriptures that speak to us from outside of ourselves. Historically, John Wesley did not name the quadrilateral as such as his theological method. There is no doubt that he turns to these four sources for his theological thinking, but he does not see them as a democracy. Wesley was acutely aware of the need for human thinking and human experience to be submitted to

God the Spirit

the word of God. Wesley scholar Albert Outler used the designation "quadrilateral" to describe Wesley's interaction with these sources, but neither Wesley nor Outler believed that tradition, reason, or experience could trump Scripture. Without Scripture as the reliable norm, we are left in a practical quandary, with no way to adjudicate claims coming from different traditioned, reasoned, and experiential perspectives.

The Witness of the Spirit

Historian David Hempton argues that "from the start, Methodism was a religion that carried the genes of dialectical tension. . . . The most pervasive was the tension between enlightenment and enthusiasm, between rational calculation and the direct inspiration of the spirit."[5] Hempton is right to see tension here, and it is a tension that gave life to the early Methodists and that ought to continue to enliven Wesleyan churches today. Wesleyan theology has long rejected false dichotomies, seeking a middle road between harmful extremes. Wesleyan churches would look very different had they opted for either reason *or* the direct inspiration of the Spirit instead of maintaining the role of both in the Christian life; and, with all the safeguards about the primacy of Scripture outlined above firmly in place, it is very significant that Wesley added, to the three accepted theological norms of his context, a fourth norm: experience. This is the vibrant genius of the Wesleyan tradition, but it is also our Achilles heel.

5. Hempton, *Methodism*, 204.

The inner witness of the Spirit was tremendously important for John Wesley and has remained so for his theological descendants. In Christ, "we cry, 'Abba! Father!'" and "it is that very Spirit bearing witness with our spirit that we are children of God" (Rom 8:15–16). The authority of experience cannot be the tyranny of individual, personal experience. Especially in our contemporary world, in which we clearly recognize that there are many different viewpoints on any given subject, granting authority to fragmented, subjective, fickle individual feelings can and does lead to disaster. But the experience Wesley claimed as a theological norm is not just any experience. It is always pneumatological. It is always the experience of the Holy Spirit in conversion, in giving us assurance that we are children of God, and the Spirit's leading us, through the means of grace, into sanctification. Wesley had responses for his critics. To those who accused the Methodists of enthusiasm, he was adamant "in rejecting fanaticism, spiritual pride, and all their congeners."[6]

Wesley insisted that, in the Christian life, we can receive "perceptible inspiration" from the Holy Spirit, and he safeguarded this by "adding a heightened emphasis on the correlation of the Spirit's witness and its genuine fruit."[7] Those who perceive the Spirit truly can be expected to bear the Spirit's fruit. Certainly, there are dangers in admitting the Spirit's work is experiential in this way, but the power of what happens when the Spirit works in our lives cannot be dismissed. Without that power, the church is a dead, weak thing, existing for itself instead of being in mission to the world. The inner witness of the

6. Outler, "Focus on the Holy Spirit," 168.
7. Ibid.

God the Spirit

Spirit makes us into witnesses, and we receive and act on the promise of Jesus that we "will receive power when the Holy Spirit has come upon you; and you will be my witnesses in Jerusalem, in all Judea and Samaria, and to the ends of the earth" (Acts 1:8).

Questions for Consideration

1. What is Karl Barth's "warning cry" to the church with respect to the Holy Spirit? What is the concern Barth's warning carries for Wesleyans? Where would Wesleyans disagree with Barth?

2. Why are Wesleyans optimistic about distinguishing truth from falsehood?

3. What are some of the resources that we as Christians can bring to bear when discerning among the "spirits"? How is this volume on the Holy Spirit a tool in this process?

4. What are the dangers of Montanism? Is it still a danger in the church today? Explain.

5. What does it mean to say that the canon is closed? What is the role of the Spirit in relationship to the canon of Scripture?

6. What concerns might arise when employing the so-called Wesleyan Quadrilateral in theological reflection? Are these concerns justified?

7. What are some of the tensions that have grown out of the Wesleyan tradition? How does the norm of experience reflect this tension in both positive and negative ways?

8. What is the witness of the Spirit? How is it related to the experience of the Spirit and the assurance of grace?
9. What connections are Wesleyans to make between the witness of the Spirit and the fruit of the Spirit? How would John Wesley want us to perceive the Spirit's presence, power, and promise in our lives?

Bibliography

Anderson, Allan. *An Introduction to Pentecostalism: Global Charismatic Christianity*. Introduction to Religion. Cambridge: Cambridge University Press, 2004.

Augustine, St. *The Confessions*. Translated by Maria Boulding. Hyde Park, NY: New City, 1997.

Barbeau, Jeffrey W. "John Wesley and the Early Church: History, Antiquity, and the Spirit of God." In *Evangelicals and the Early Church: Recovery, Reform, Renewal*, edited by George Kalantzis and Andrew Tooley, 52–76. Eugene, OR: Cascade, 2012.

Barth, Karl. *Church Dogmatics* II.1, *The Doctrine of God*. Translated by G. T. Thomson et al. Edited by G. W. Bromiley and T. F. Torrance. Edinburgh: T. & T. Clark, 1957.

Basil the Great, St. *On the Holy Spirit*. Translated by David Anderson. Popular Patristics Series 5. Crestwood, NY: St. Vladimir's Seminary Press, 1980.

BeDuhn, Jason. *The Manichaean Body: In Discipline and Ritual*. Baltimore: Johns Hopkins University Press, 2002.

Bonhoeffer, Dietrich. *The Cost of Discipleship*. Translated by R. H. Fuller. New York: Simon and Schuster, 1995.

Brand, Chad Owen, ed. *Perspectives on Spirit Baptism: Five Views*. Nashville: Broadman & Holman, 2004.

Bromiley, G. W. "Filioque." In *Evangelical Dictionary of Theology*, edited by Walter A. Elwell, 452. 2nd ed. Grand Rapids: Baker, 2001.

Chan, Francis. *Forgotten God: Reversing Our Tragic Neglect of the Holy Spirit*. Colorado Springs: Cook, 2009.

Collins, Kenneth J. *The Scripture Way of Salvation: The Heart of John Wesley's Theology*. Nashville: Abingdon, 1997.

Cox, Harvey. *Fire from Heaven: The Rise of Pentecostal Spirituality and the Reshaping of Religion in the 21st Century*. Cambridge: Da Capo, 2001.

Bibliography

Donne, John. "Holy Sonnet 11 (XV)." In *John Donne's Poetry*, selected and edited by Arthur L. Clements, 116. 2nd ed. New York: Norton, 1992.

Fee, Gordon D. *God's Empowering Presence: The Holy Spirit in the Letters of Paul*. Peabody, MA: Hendrickson, 1994.

Gregory of Nazianzus, St. "The Fourth Theological Oration." In *Nicene and Post-Nicene Fathers*, Second Series, vol. 7, translated by Charles Gordon Browne and James Edward Swallow, edited by Philip Schaff and Henry Wace, 309–18. Peabody, MA: Hendrickson, 1994.

Gregory of Nyssa, St. "On the Holy Spirit: Against the Followers of Macedonius." In *Nicene and Post-Nicene Fathers*, Second Series, vol. 5, translated by William Moore and Henry Austin, edited by Philip Schaff and Henry Wace, 315–25. Peabody, MA: Hendrickson, 1994.

Grenz, Stanley J. *Theology for the Community of God*. Grand Rapids: Eerdmans, 2000.

Gutiérrez, Gustavo. *A Theology of Liberation: History, Politics and Salvation*. Translated and edited by Caridad Inda and John Eagleson. Maryknoll, NY: Orbis, 1988.

Hempton, David. *Methodism: Empire of the Spirit*. New Haven: Yale University Press, 2005.

Hindmarsh, Bruce. *The Evangelical Conversion Narrative: Spiritual Autobiography in Early Modern England*. Oxford: Oxford University Press, 2005.

Jacobsen, Douglas G. *Thinking in the Spirit: Theologies of the Early Pentecostal Movement*. Bloomington: Indiana University Press, 2003.

Jenkins, Phillip. *The New Faces of Christianity: Believing the Bible in the Global South*. Oxford: Oxford University Press, 2006.

Jenson, Robert. "The Father, He . . ." In *Speaking the Christian God: The Holy Trinity and the Challenge of Feminism*, edited by Alvin F. Kimel Jr., 95–109. Grand Rapids: Eerdmans, 1992.

Jones, Beth Felker. *Marks of His Wounds: Gender Politics and Bodily Resurrection*. Oxford: Oxford University Press, 2007.

Maddox, Randy L. *Responsible Grace: John Wesley's Practical Theology*. Nashville: Abingdon, 1994.

McGrath, Alister. *Iustitia Dei: A History of the Christian Doctrine of Justification*. 3rd ed. Cambridge: Cambridge University Press, 2005.

Miles, Margaret R. *The Word Made Flesh: A History of Christian Thought*. Malden, MA: Blackwell, 2005.

Bibliography

Miley, John. "The Agency of the Spirit." In *Leading Wesleyan Thinkers*, edited by Richard S. Taylor, 3:208–11. Great Holiness Classics. Kansas City: Beacon Hill, 1985.

———. *Systematic Theology*. Vol. 2. New York: Hunt & Eaton, 1984.

Oden, Thomas C. *Classic Christianity: A Systematic Theology*. New York: HarperCollins, 1992.

Outler, Albert C. "A Focus on the Holy Spirit: Spirit and Spirituality in John Wesley." In *The Wesleyan Theological Heritage: Essays of Albert C. Outler*, edited by Thomas C. Oden and Leicester R. Longden, 159–73. Grand Rapids: Zondervan, 1991.

Peters, John Leland. *Christian Perfection and American Methodism*. Grand Rapids: Zondervan, 1985.

Pinnock, Clark. *Flame of Love: A Theology of the Holy Spirit*. Downers Grove, IL: InterVarsity, 1999.

Rogers, Eugene F., Jr. *After the Spirit: A Constructive Pneumatology from Resources Outside the Modern West*. Radical Traditions. Grand Rapids: Eerdmans, 2005.

Rowe, Christopher Kavin. *World Upside Down: Reading Acts in the Graeco-Roman Age*. New York: Oxford University Press, 2009.

Rudolph, Kurt. *Gnosis: The Nature and History of Gnosticism*. San Francisco: HarperOne, 1987.

Sanneh, Lamin O. *Disciples of All Nations: Pillars of World Christainity*. Studies in World Christianity. New York: Oxford University Press, 2007.

Smith, Christian. "On 'Moralistic Therapeutic Deism' as U.S. Teenagers' Actual, Tacit, De Facto Religious Faith." In *Religion and Youth*, edited by Sylvia Collins-Mayo and P. Dandelion, 41–46. Theology and Religion in Interdisciplinary Perspective Series. Aldershot, UK: Ashgate, 2010.

Soskice, Janet Martin. *The Kindness of God: Metaphor, Gender, and Religious Language*. Oxford: Oxford University Press, 2007.

Tanner, Kathryn. *Jesus, Humanity, and the Trinity: A Brief Systematic Theology*. Minneapolis: Fortress, 2001.

Wainwright, Geoffrey. *Doxology: The Praise of God in Worship, Doctrine, and Life: A Systematic Theology*. New York: Oxford University Press, 1980.

Webster, John. *Holiness*. Grand Rapids: Eerdmans, 2003.

Wesley, Charles. "Hymn XIV, 'Why will ye die, O house of Israel?'" In *The Poetical Works of John and Charles Wesley*, 3:85. London: Wesleyan-Methodist Conference Office, 1869.

———. "Love Divine, All Loves Excelling." In *The United Methodist Hymnal: Book of United Methodist Worship*, 384. Nashville: United Methodist Publishing House, 1989.

Bibliography

———. "Universal Redemption." In *The Poetical Works of John and Charles Wesley*, 1:308–15. London: Wesleyan-Methodist Conference Office, 1869.

Wesley, John. "Biblical Promises of Perfection" (1747). In *The John Wesley Reader on Christian Perfection, 1725–1791*, edited by Mark K. Olson, 167–69. Fenwick, MI: Truth in Heart, 2008.

———. "Catholic Spirit (Sermon 39)." In *The Works of John Wesley: Sermons*, edited by John Emory, 1:346–55. New York: Eaton & Mains, 1825.

———. *Explanatory Notes upon the New Testament*. Vol. 1, *Matthew to Acts*. Grand Rapids: Baker, 1981.

———. "The More Excellent Way." In *John Wesley's Sermons: An Anthology*, edited by Albert C. Outler and Richard P. Heitzenrater, 511–21. Nashville: Abingdon, 1991.

———. "On Original Sin (Sermon 20)." In *John Wesley's Sermons: An Anthology*, edited by Albert C. Outler and Richard P. Heitzenrater, 326–34. Nashville: Abingdon, 1991.

———. "On Perfection" (1784). In *The John Wesley Reader on Christian Perfection, 1725–1791*, edited by Mark K. Olson, 274–90. Fenwick, MI: Truth in Heart, 2008.

———. "The Scripture Way of Salvation." In *John Wesley's Sermons: An Anthology*, edited by Albert C. Outler and Richard P. Heitzenrater, 372–80. Nashville: Abingdon, 1991.

———. "The Unity of the Divine Being." In *John Wesley's Sermons: An Anthology*, edited by Albert C. Outler and Richard P. Heitzenrater, 532–39. Nashville: Abingdon, 1991.

———. Wesley to Miss Furly, June 14, 1757. In *The John Wesley Reader on Christian Perfection, 1725–1791*, edited by Mark K. Olson, 191–93. Fenwick, MI: Truth in Heart, 2008.

———. Wesley to Richard Morgan Sr., January 14, 1734. In *The John Wesley Reader on Christian Perfection, 1725–1791*, edited by Mark K. Olson, 38. Fenwick, MI: Truth in Heart, 2008.

Young, Frances M. *The Making of the Creeds*. Philadelphia: Trinity, 1991.

www.ingramcontent.com/pod-product-compliance
Lightning Source LLC
Chambersburg PA
CBHW070334100426
42812CB00005B/1334